HSPT EXAM PREP: Your Strategic Playbook for Success

Introduction

Welcome to "Conquering Catholic High School Entrance Exams: Your Strategic Playbook for Success." This book is your ally in navigating the challenging journey towards Catholic high school admission. Our mission? To demystify the often intimidating process of preparing for Catholic high school entrance exams and to equip you with strategies for success.

Embarking on the path to Catholic high school can feel daunting. The entrance exams, a critical component of this journey, often seem shrouded in mystery and complexity. But fear not! This book is designed to transform that uncertainty into confidence. Here, we unravel the complexities of these exams, presenting them in a clear, understandable, and actionable format.

We believe in a straightforward, informative, yet engaging approach. Each chapter is crafted to be both accessible and practical, ensuring you not only understand the material but can also apply it effectively.

Our playbook is more than just a study guide. It's a comprehensive resource that combines essential knowledge with effective strategies.

From understanding the structure and content of the exams to practice exams, we cover it all. The tips and insights provided are based on extensive research and proven methodologies, ensuring you're receiving reliable and valuable guidance.

Remember, conquering these exams is not just about memorizing facts or mastering test-taking skills. It's about developing the confidence and resilience that will serve you well in high school and beyond. We're excited to be part of your journey and are committed to helping you achieve your goals.

Together, let's turn this challenge into an opportunity for growth and success. Let's conquer the Catholic high school entrance exams!

Success Story

As someone who has navigated the intricate world of Catholic high school entrance exams, I understand the challenges and anxieties they bring. Through this book, I aim to share not just strategies but also inspiration, drawing from a journey that transformed challenges into triumph.

Let me share a story that mirrors the experiences of many students I have worked with. Meet Emily, a bright and ambitious student, eager to attend her dream Catholic high school. Like many, Emily found herself overwhelmed by the prospect of the entrance exams. The pressure of performing well, coupled with the fear of not meeting expectations, cast a shadow of doubt on her abilities.

Emily's journey, however, turned around when she realized that success on these exams was not just about hard work, but smart work. Through a structured approach, emphasizing understanding over rote memorization and strategy over endless practice, Emily transformed her preparation. She learned to tackle each section of the exam with a clear plan, manage her time efficiently, and maintain a positive mindset.

The result? Not only did Emily score exceptionally well, but she also gained a newfound confidence that propelled her forward in her academic journey. Her success story is a testament to the fact that with the right approach, guidance, and mindset, conquering these exams is not just a possibility but a certainty.

As the author of this book and your guide, I bring a wealth of experience in preparing students for these pivotal exams. I have seen firsthand the common struggles and the unique challenges each student faces. This book is a culmination of years of research, teaching, and feedback, tailored to address every aspect of the entrance exam preparation.

My goal is to make your journey towards Catholic high school as successful as Emily's. Whether it's understanding complex topics, mastering test-taking strategies, or overcoming anxiety, this book has got you covered. Together, we will navigate this path, turning potential obstacles into stepping stones for success.

Let's embark on this journey together, armed with knowledge, strategies, and the inspiration to conquer!

Chapter 1: The HSPT (High School Placement Test)

The High School Placement Test (HSPT) is a comprehensive assessment used by many Catholic high schools for admission purposes. It typically covers five main areas: Verbal Skills, Quantitative Skills, Reading Comprehension, Mathematics, and Language. The HSPT is known for its broad range of questions, testing everything from analogies and logic to problem-solving and arithmetic. It's a timed test, usually taking about 2.5 hours to complete.

Personalized Study Plan

Understanding the format and timing of the exam you are preparing for is crucial. Once you have a grasp of the exam's structure, the next step is to conduct an initial self-assessment. This assessment helps identify your strengths and areas for improvement, forming the basis of your personalized study plan.

A well-tailored study plan takes into account your unique learning style, the time you have until the exam, and the specific requirements of the test you'll be taking. Whether it's the broad-ranging content of the HSPT, the inference-focused questions of the COOP, or the reasoning and expression elements of the TACHS, your study plan should reflect the specific demands of your target exam.

In the following chapters, we'll delve into how to create and adjust this study plan, mastering each section of your chosen exam, and strategies to maximize your performance.

Understanding the Format and Timing of the Exam

Welcome to a crucial aspect of your exam preparation journey: understanding the format and timing of the HSPT exam. This knowledge is not just a foundational step in your study plan; it's a strategic advantage. Here's why:

The Power of Familiarity

Being familiar with the exam format - the types of questions, the sections involved, and their order - reduces surprises on test day. This familiarity breeds confidence, allowing you to approach the test with a calm, focused mindset.

Effective Time Management

The exam has its own time constraints. Knowing how much time you have for each section enables you to develop effective time management skills. By practicing under these time limits, you can pace yourself appropriately, ensuring that you have enough time to address every question.

Tailored Study Approach

Understanding the structure of the exam helps in tailoring your study approach. For instance, if a test has a heavy emphasis on math, you'll know to allocate more study time to that subject. Similarly, if an exam includes an essay section, you can prepare accordingly by practicing your writing skills.

Optimizing Performance

The timing of each section can impact your performance. If a particular section of the exam is longer or more complex, knowing this in advance allows you to prepare mentally and physically for the endurance required.

Reducing Anxiety

Exam anxiety often stems from fear of the unknown. By familiarizing yourself with the exam format and timing, you demystify the test, reducing anxiety and improving your overall performance.

Strategic Question Approach

Different exams have different penalties for wrong answers. Knowing whether to guess on a question or leave it blank is part of understanding the exam's format and can significantly impact your score.

Realistic Practice Exams

Finally, understanding the format and timing is crucial when taking realistic practice exams. These practice sessions are essential for applying what you've learned, testing your knowledge under exam-like conditions, and further refining your time management skills.

Remember, knowledge is power. The more you know about your enemy - in this case, the entrance exams - the better equipped you are to conquer them.

Crafting Your Personalized Study Plan: The Role of Initial Self-Assessment

Embarking on the journey to conquer Catholic high school entrance exams calls for more than just hard work; it demands smart work. A critical component of this smart approach is developing a personalized study plan, which begins with an initial self-assessment. Let's dive into why this self-assessment is vital and how it can shape your study plan.

The Importance of Initial Self-Assessment

Self-assessment serves as your academic mirror. It reflects your current capabilities, highlighting your strengths and pinpointing areas that require more attention. This honest evaluation is crucial because:

1. Identifies Knowledge Gaps: Understanding what you already know and what you need to focus on saves time and directs your efforts efficiently.
2. Helps Set Realistic Goals: Knowing your starting point allows you to set achievable goals and track your progress effectively.
3. Customizes Your Learning: Every student is unique. A personalized study plan caters to your individual learning style and pace.
4. Boosts Confidence: Familiarity with your strengths enhances self-confidence, a crucial element during exam preparation.

Creating Your Personalized Study Plan

Once you've assessed your skills and identified areas for improvement, the next step is to create a study plan tailored to your needs. This plan should be:

1. Balanced: It should allocate time for all subjects, with more focus on areas needing improvement.
2. Flexible: Your plan must adapt as you progress. Regular reviews and adjustments are key.
3. Realistic: Set attainable goals and deadlines that motivate rather than overwhelm you.

4. Comprehensive: Include time for reviewing concepts, practicing questions, and taking full-length practice exams.

Implementation and Adaptation

Putting your study plan into action requires discipline and consistency. However, be prepared to adapt. If certain strategies aren't working, or if you find some topics more challenging than expected, adjust your plan accordingly. Continuous adaptation ensures that your study plan remains effective and relevant throughout your preparation journey.

In the following chapters, we will explore specific strategies and tips for each exam section, further aiding in refining your personalized study plan. Remember, a plan that evolves with you is a plan that leads to success.

Your personalized study plan is not just a schedule; it's a roadmap to achieving your academic goals. Embark on this journey with confidence, knowing that you're preparing in a way that best suits you.

In the next chapter we'll talk about your custom study blueprint.

Chapter 2: Custom Study Blueprint

Creating a Study Plan from Your Initial Assessment: A Step-by-Step Guide

After completing your initial self-assessment, the next crucial step is to transform those insights into an actionable and effective study plan. This chapter outlines a step-by-step process to craft a study blueprint that works uniquely for you.

Step 1: Analyze Your Assessment Results

Start by reviewing your self-assessment results carefully. Identify which subjects or topics you are comfortable with and which ones require more attention. Pay attention to patterns; are there specific types of questions you consistently struggle with? This analysis forms the backbone of your personalized study plan.

Step 2: Set Specific Goals

Based on your analysis, set clear and specific goals for each area of improvement. These goals should be SMART: Specific, Measurable, Achievable, Relevant, and Time-bound. For instance, rather than a vague goal like "improve in math," set a specific target like "increase math practice test scores by 10% in the next four weeks."

Step 3: Allocate Study Time Wisely

Now, divide your study time. Allocate more time to areas that require the most improvement, but don't neglect your stronger subjects. A balanced approach is key. If, for example, math is a weak point, you might allocate 40% of your study time to it, 30% to verbal skills, and the rest divided among other areas.

Step 4: Choose Study Methods and Materials

Select study methods and materials that cater to your learning style. This might include textbooks, online resources, practice exams, or interactive tools. If you're a visual learner, incorporate charts and diagrams. If you learn better by doing, focus on practice questions and problem-solving exercises.

Step 5: Schedule Regular Reviews

Incorporate regular review sessions into your plan. These sessions should focus on revisiting previously studied topics to reinforce learning and assess progress.

Step 6: Plan for Practice Tests

Practice tests are crucial. Schedule them regularly to simulate the exam experience and track your progress. Use these tests to adjust your study plan as needed. Initially, you might take a practice test every two weeks, gradually increasing the frequency as the exam approaches.

Step 7: Adapt and Evolve

Your study plan should be a living document. Regularly assess your progress and be prepared to make adjustments. If you find that you're progressing faster in one area, reallocate time to focus on weaker sections.

Step 8: Include Breaks and Self-Care

Finally, ensure your plan includes breaks and time for self-care. Consistent studying is important, but so is maintaining your overall well-being.

Adjusting Your Study Plan as You Progress

Progress is not always a straight line, especially when preparing for something as crucial as Catholic high school entrance exams. As you move forward, your study plan will need to evolve to reflect your growing knowledge, changing needs, and any unforeseen challenges. Here's how you can effectively adjust your study plan as you progress.

Tip 1: Regularly Review Your Progress

Set aside time each week to review what you've learned and how you've performed in practice tests. This review will help you identify if certain areas are improving or if there are new topics where you need more focus.

Tip 2: Be Flexible with Time Allocation

If you find that you're excelling in a subject quicker than expected, it might be time to reallocate some of that study time to areas where progress is slower. Flexibility is key; don't stick rigidly to a plan if your needs have changed.

Tip 3: Adapt to Learning Styles and Preferences

As you study, you'll likely discover certain methods that work better for you than others. Whether it's visual aids, interactive exercises, or reading and summarizing, adjust your plan to incorporate more of these effective strategies.

Tip 4: Use Practice Tests as Milestones

Regular practice tests are not just for assessing knowledge; they're also for evaluating your study plan. Based on your performance, you might decide to spend more time on test-taking strategies or revisit foundational concepts.

Tip 5: Address New Challenges

Sometimes, new challenges emerge as you delve deeper into subjects. If you encounter a topic that's unexpectedly difficult, don't hesitate to modify your plan to include additional study resources or seek extra help in that area.

Tip 6: Stay Attuned to Your Well-being

If your current study routine is causing stress or fatigue, it's crucial to adjust. This could mean scheduling more frequent breaks, changing your study environment, or finding ways to make studying more enjoyable and less stressful.

Tip 7: Involve Others in Your Progress

Don't forget to involve a teacher, tutor, or even a family member in your progress reviews. They can provide valuable external perspectives and may suggest adjustments you hadn't considered.

Tip 8: Be Open to Revisiting Previously Mastered Content

Even if you've mastered a topic, it's beneficial to revisit it occasionally to ensure that your understanding remains sharp. This is particularly true for subjects that build upon previously learned material.

Striking the Right Balance: Focused Study and Healthy Breaks

In the journey towards acing your Catholic high school entrance exams, maintaining a balance between dedicated study time and healthy breaks is essential. This section is dedicated to helping you strike that perfect balance. After all, effective studying isn't just about the hours you put in; it's also about how you use those hours and the quality of your breaks.

The Role of Focused Study

Focused study is undeniably crucial. It's during these times that you dive deep into subjects, grapple with challenging concepts, and build your knowledge. However, the key is to ensure that this time is used effectively:

1. Quality Over Quantity: Aim for high-quality study sessions rather than just long hours. This means creating a distraction-free environment and having a clear goal for each study session.

2. Active Learning: Engage actively with the material. This could be through problem-solving, teaching the content to someone else, or applying concepts to different scenarios.

3. Regular Review: Regularly revisit previous topics to reinforce your learning and ensure retention.

The Importance of Healthy Breaks

Breaks are not just downtime; they are an integral part of your learning process. They help in:

1. Mental Rejuvenation: Breaks allow your brain to rest and consolidate information. A short walk, a nap, or even a change of scenery can rejuvenate your mind.

2. Preventing Burnout: Regular breaks help prevent study fatigue and burnout, ensuring you can study more effectively in the long run.

3. Enhancing Creativity: Sometimes, stepping away from the books can provide a new perspective, helping you solve a problem or grasp a concept that was challenging earlier.

To find your ideal balance, consider:

1. Pomodoro Technique: Try studying for 25 minutes, then taking a 5-minute break. After four such sessions, take a longer break of 15-30 minutes.

2. Vary Your Activities: During breaks, engage in activities that are different from studying. Physical activities, hobbies, or even just relaxing can be beneficial.

3. Listen to Your Body: Pay attention to your concentration levels. If you find your focus waning, it might be time for a break.

4. Flexible Scheduling: Some days you might be able to focus longer, while on others, you might need more frequent breaks. Be flexible and adjust accordingly.

In the next chapter we'll talk about how to master verbal skills for exams and interviews.

Chapter 3: Verbal Mastery

Mastering the Essentials of Verbal Skills for Catholic High School Entrance Exams

In this section, we delve into the heart of verbal skills essential for excelling in the Catholic high school entrance exams: vocabulary, grammar, and comprehension. These skills are not just crucial for the test but are foundational for your overall academic and personal development.

Vocabulary: The Building Blocks of Communication

Vocabulary is more than just a list of words; it's the toolset for expressing ideas, understanding others, and engaging with complex texts.

1. Develop a Reading Habit: Regular reading exposes you to a wide range of words in context, enhancing your understanding and recall.
2. Use Vocabulary Lists: Focus on lists specifically curated for the HSPT, COOP, and TACHS exams. Make flashcards or use apps to reinforce learning.
3. Contextual Learning: Learn new words in the context of sentences or stories, which aids in better retention and understanding of nuances.

Grammar: The Framework of Effective Expression

Grammar is the set of rules that organizes and gives meaning to our words and sentences. A strong grasp of grammar is essential for clear and effective communication.

1. Understand Core Concepts: Focus on understanding basic grammatical concepts like parts of speech, sentence structure, tense, agreement, and punctuation.
2. Practice Through Writing: Regular writing exercises can improve your grammatical skills. Write short essays, summaries, or journals.

3. Review and Apply: Review grammar rules regularly and apply them in practice questions. Pay special attention to common grammatical errors.

Comprehension: Interpreting and Understanding Texts

Comprehension skills are crucial for understanding, analyzing, and interpreting the reading material, an essential component of entrance exams.

1. Practice Active Reading: Engage actively with the text by summarizing, questioning, and predicting. Annotating texts can also enhance understanding.
2. Understand the Types of Questions: Familiarize yourself with the types of comprehension questions typically found in the exams, like main idea, inference, and detail questions.
3. Develop Critical Thinking: Go beyond the text to analyze and evaluate information. Ask yourself what the author is trying to convey and why.

Applying Your Skills: Targeted Exercises for Vocabulary, Grammar, and Comprehension

To truly master the verbal section of the Catholic high school entrance exams, it's not enough to just understand the concepts; you need to apply them. This section provides targeted exercises designed to strengthen your vocabulary, grammar, and comprehension skills, focusing on practical application.

Vocabulary Exercises

1. Word-In-Context: For each new word you learn, write a sentence using it in context. This helps solidify understanding and usage.
2. Synonyms and Antonyms: Create a list of synonyms and antonyms for each new word. This broadens your understanding and prepares you for questions that test these areas.
3. Daily Word Challenge: Challenge yourself to learn and use a new word every day. This consistent practice builds vocabulary over time.

Grammar Exercises

1. Sentence Correction: Practice correcting sentences with common grammatical errors. This sharpens your ability to identify and fix mistakes.
2. Grammar in Writing: Regularly write short essays or paragraphs. Focus on using varied sentence structures and correct grammar. Review and revise your writing to improve.

3. Grammar Quizzes: Take advantage of online grammar quizzes and exercises. These provide immediate feedback and cover a range of topics.

Comprehension Exercises

1. Reading and Summarizing: Read a short article and write a summary. Focus on capturing the main idea and key details.
2. Question-Answer Relationship (QAR): Practice QAR strategies by identifying 'Right There' (literal) and 'Think and Search' (inferential) questions in your reading.
3. Critical Analysis: For each reading passage, write down a critical analysis. What is the author's purpose? What are the underlying themes?

Practice Questions with Explanations

To further enhance your verbal skills for the Catholic high school entrance exams, let's dive into some practice questions. These questions cover vocabulary, grammar, and comprehension, with clear explanations to help you understand the reasoning behind each answer.

Vocabulary Questions

1. Question: Choose the word that best completes the sentence: "The lawyer's argument was so _____ that it left no doubt about the innocence of her client."
  - A) ambiguous
  - B) convoluted
  - C) lucid
  - D) redundant

  Answer: C) lucid
  Explanation: 'Lucid' means clear and easy to understand. In this context, a clear argument would leave no doubt, making 'lucid' the correct choice.

2. Question: Select the antonym of the word "benevolent."
  - A) Malevolent
  - B) Generous
  - C) Kind-hearted
  - D) Charitable

  Answer: A) Malevolent
  Explanation: 'Benevolent' means showing kindness or goodwill. Therefore, 'malevolent,' which means having or showing a wish to do evil, is its antonym.

Grammar Questions

1. Question: Identify the error in the sentence: "She has fewer apples, but more oranges than I do."

- A) Use of 'fewer'
- B) Use of 'more'
- C) No error
- D) Comma usage

Answer: C) No error
Explanation: The sentence correctly uses 'fewer' for countable items (apples) and 'more' for countable items (oranges). There is no grammatical error.

2. Question: Choose the correctly punctuated sentence.

- A) Although, he was late he managed to catch the train.
- B) Although he was late, he managed to catch the train.
- C) Although he was late; he managed to catch the train.
- D) Although, he was late; he managed to catch the train.

Answer: B) Although he was late, he managed to catch the train.
Explanation: The correct sentence is B. The comma after 'late' correctly separates the dependent clause at the beginning from the independent clause.

Comprehension Questions

1. Question: Read the following passage: "The solar panels installed on the roof will significantly reduce the building's energy costs. Moreover, they are an environmentally friendly solution to energy consumption." What is the main idea of the passage?
   - A) The installation of solar panels is expensive.
   - B) Solar panels will cut energy costs and are environmentally friendly.
   - C) The building has high energy costs.
   - D) Solar panels are used for energy consumption.

   Answer: B) Solar panels will cut energy costs and are environmentally friendly.
   Explanation: The passage focuses on the benefits of solar panels, which include reducing energy costs and being environmentally friendly.

In the next chapter we'll talk about strategies for navigating your way through the mathematics questions.

Chapter 4: Mathematical Strategies

Grasping Key Math Concepts: Arithmetic, Algebra, and Geometry

While the verbal section is crucial, a solid grasp of math concepts is equally important for Catholic high school entrance exams. This section provides a concise summary of the key math areas you need to be familiar with: arithmetic, algebra, and geometry. Let's break these down to ensure you have a strong foundation.

Arithmetic: The Backbone of Math

Arithmetic is the most fundamental branch of mathematics, and it forms the basis for many of the problems you'll encounter on the exams.

1. Basic Operations: Ensure you are comfortable with addition, subtraction, multiplication, and division. Speed and accuracy are vital.
2. Fractions and Decimals: Understand how to work with fractions and decimals, including conversion between the two and operations involving each.
3. Percentages: Grasp how to calculate percentages, as well as how to use percentages in various contexts, like discounts or interest rates.

Algebra: The Language of Unknowns

Algebra introduces you to the concept of using letters and symbols to represent numbers and quantities in equations and formulas.

1. Variables and Expressions: Get comfortable with variables and learn how to manipulate algebraic expressions.
2. Equations and Inequalities: Know how to solve linear equations and inequalities, and understand the principles behind them.
3. Word Problems: Practice translating real-world situations into algebraic expressions and equations.

Geometry: The World of Shapes and Sizes

Geometry deals with the properties and relations of points, lines, surfaces, and solids.

1. Basic Shapes and Properties: Familiarize yourself with the properties of basic shapes like triangles, rectangles, and circles.
2. Perimeter, Area, and Volume: Learn how to calculate the perimeter, area, and volume of various shapes.
3. Angles and Their Relationships: Understand the different types of angles and their relationships, including complementary, supplementary, and vertical angles.

for these exams. APA citations are not included as the content is specifically created for the book's context.*

Efficient Problem-Solving: Strategies and Shortcuts

Mastering math is as much about understanding concepts as it is about solving problems efficiently. This section of the book focuses on strategies and shortcuts that can help you tackle math problems more effectively and efficiently in your Catholic high school entrance exams.

Breaking Down the Problem

1. Understand Before Solving: Before diving into solving a problem, take a moment to fully understand what is being asked. Identify the knowns, the unknowns, and what the problem is asking you to find.
2. Simplify the Problem: Break complex problems into smaller, manageable parts. Solve each part step by step, then combine these solutions to solve the overall problem.
3. Draw Diagrams: For geometry problems, a simple diagram can often make the problem clearer and easier to solve.

Using Mathematical Shortcuts

1. Mental Math: Develop your mental math skills. Being able to quickly perform basic calculations in your head saves time and keeps you focused on the larger problem.
2. Estimation: Sometimes, particularly for multiple-choice questions, estimation can help you quickly eliminate wrong answers and narrow down your choices.
3. Algebraic Shortcuts: Familiarize yourself with common algebraic formulas and shortcuts, like the quadratic formula or factoring techniques.

Tackling Common Problem Types

1. Word Problems: Translate the words into mathematical language. Look for keywords that indicate mathematical operations, such as 'total' for addition or 'per' for division.
2. Pattern Recognition: Many math problems, especially in algebra and geometry, are about recognizing and applying patterns. Practice identifying these patterns.
3. Checking Your Work: If time permits, use a different method to check your answer. This can be especially helpful in algebra, where you can substitute your solution back into the original equation.

Time Management

1. Prioritize Questions: Tackle the problems you find easiest first. This boosts confidence and ensures you secure these points early on.
2. Time Allocation: Keep an eye on the clock. Don't spend too much time on any single problem. If you're stuck, move on and come back to it if time permits.

Math Practice Questions with Step-by-Step Solutions

To solidify your understanding and application of key math concepts, let's dive into some practice questions. These questions span arithmetic, algebra, and geometry, and come with detailed step-by-step solutions to enhance your learning process.

Arithmetic Question

Question: If a sweater is discounted by 25% and the sale price is $45, what was the original price?

Solution:
1. Let the original price be x.

2. The discount is 25%, so the sale price represents 75% of the original price: $0.75x$.
3. Set up the equation: $0.75x = 45$.
4. Solve for x by dividing both sides by 0.75: $x = \frac{45}{0.75} = 60$.
5. So, the original price of the sweater was $60.

Algebra Question

Question: Solve for x in the equation $2x + 3 = 11$.

Solution:
1. Start by subtracting 3 from both sides: $2x + 3 - 3 = 11 - 3$.
2. This simplifies to $2x = 8$.
3. Now, divide both sides by 2: $\frac{2x}{2} = \frac{8}{2}$.
4. This gives $x = 4$.

Geometry Question

Question: Find the area of a triangle with a base of 10 cm and a height of 5 cm.

Solution:
1. The formula for the area of a triangle is $\frac{1}{2} \times \text{base} \times \text{height}$.
2. Plug in the values: $\frac{1}{2} \times 10 \times 5$.

3. Calculate: $5 \times 5 = 25$.
4. So, the area of the triangle is 25 cm².

In the next chapter we'll talk about how to enhance your reading and comprehension.

Chapter 5: Reading For Understanding

Enhancing Reading Comprehension: Quick and Effective Techniques

Reading comprehension is a critical skill for Catholic high school entrance exams and beyond. It's not just about reading the words; it's about understanding, interpreting, and analyzing them. This section focuses on techniques to improve your reading comprehension quickly and effectively.

Skimming and Scanning

1. Skimming: This is the technique of quickly going over the text to get a general idea of the content. Look

for main ideas rather than details. Focus on headings, topic sentences, and summary paragraphs.

2. Scanning: Use this when looking for specific information. Move your eyes quickly over the text until you find the specific piece of information you need.

Active Reading

1. Engage with the Text: As you read, think about what the author is trying to convey. Ask yourself questions about the content and its purpose.

2. Make Predictions: Based on the heading and introductory paragraph, try to predict what the passage might be about. This sets a purpose for reading and keeps you engaged.

Note-Taking and Highlighting

1. Key Points: While reading, note down or highlight key points. This helps in retaining important information and is useful for quick revisions.

2. Margin Notes: Write questions or summarize sections in the margins. This keeps you active and engaged with the material.

Understanding Context

1. Contextual Clues: Pay attention to the context in which words are used. This can help you understand

the meaning of unfamiliar words or complex sentences.

2. Inference: Practice making inferences – reading between the lines to understand what is implied but not directly stated.

Visualization

1. Create Mental Images: Try to visualize the scenarios or concepts described in the text. This can be particularly helpful for narrative passages or complex descriptions.

2. Linking with Prior Knowledge: Relate the content to what you already know or have experienced. This makes the material more relatable and easier to comprehend.

Strategies for Tackling Various Types of Reading Passages

Reading comprehension on Catholic high school entrance exams often includes a variety of passage types, each requiring a slightly different approach. Understanding how to tackle each type can greatly enhance your ability to comprehend and interpret the material effectively. Let's explore strategies tailored for different types of reading passages.

Narrative Passages

Narrative passages, often excerpts from novels or short stories, primarily test your ability to understand plot, character development, and theme.

1. Identify the Plot: Focus on the sequence of events. Try to understand the cause-and-effect relationship between different events.
2. Analyze Characters: Pay attention to the descriptions of characters, their actions, and their interactions. This can give insights into their personalities and motivations.
3. Look for Themes: Try to discern the underlying message or theme of the narrative. This could be a moral lesson, a commentary on society, or an exploration of a particular emotion or experience.

Expository Passages

Expository texts are informative and factual, commonly found in textbooks, articles, and essays. They aim to explain or inform about a topic.

1. Identify Main Ideas and Details: Focus on understanding the main idea of each paragraph and how the details support it.

2. Understand the Structure: Recognize the organization of the text – is it cause and effect, comparison and contrast, or problem and solution?
3. Note-Taking: Writing down key points can help in understanding and remembering the information presented.

Persuasive Passages

Persuasive texts aim to convince the reader of the author's point of view. They often include arguments and opinions.

1. Identify the Argument: What is the author trying to convince you of? Understanding the main argument is crucial.
2. Evaluate Evidence: Look at the evidence the author presents to support their argument. Is it strong and logical?
3. Recognize Persuasive Techniques: Authors may use emotional appeals, logical reasoning, or ethical arguments to persuade readers. Recognizing these techniques can help you better understand the author's strategy.

Poetry

Poetry can be challenging due to its use of metaphor, imagery, and sometimes abstract concepts.

1. Identify the Theme: Try to understand the overall theme or message of the poem.
2. Analyze Language and Structure: Pay attention to the poet's choice of words, the use of rhyme and rhythm, and the structure of the poem.
3. Interpret Imagery and Symbols: Poets often use imagery and symbols to convey deeper meanings. Try to interpret what these could signify in the context of the poem.

Practice Reading Passages with Questions and Explanations

To enhance your reading comprehension skills, this section includes a practice reading passage followed by questions. This exercise is designed to mimic the style of passages you might encounter in Catholic high school entrance exams, complete with thorough explanations for each question.

Practice Passage

In the heart of the Amazon rainforest, a unique ecosystem thrives. The dense canopy of towering trees creates a lush, green world where sunlight struggles to touch the ground. This vibrant rainforest is home to a staggering variety of species, many of which are not found anywhere else on Earth. However, this precious habitat faces numerous threats, including deforestation, climate change, and pollution, which pose significant challenges to its survival.

Questions

1. What is the main idea of the passage?
   A) The Amazon rainforest is a challenging place to live.
   B) The Amazon rainforest is home to a variety of species.
   C) The Amazon rainforest faces several threats to its survival.
   D) The canopy in the Amazon rainforest is very dense.

   Answer: C) The Amazon rainforest faces several threats to its survival.

Explanation: While the passage mentions the diversity of species and the dense canopy, the main focus is on the threats facing the rainforest, making option C the correct answer.

2. According to the passage, why is the Amazon rainforest unique?
   A) It has a dense canopy.

B) It is home to many species not found elsewhere.

C) It is in the heart of the Amazon.

D) It struggles with sunlight.

Answer: B) It is home to many species not found elsewhere.

Explanation: The passage specifically states that the rainforest is home to a "staggering variety of species, many of which are not found anywhere else on Earth," which makes option B the correct answer.

3. What can be inferred about the Amazon rainforest?

   A) It has adapted well to climate change.

   B) It is larger than other rainforests.

   C) It is under threat but still thriving.

   D) It receives a lot of sunlight.

   Answer: C) It is under threat but still thriving.

Explanation: The passage mentions the threats faced by the rainforest but also describes its vibrant ecosystem, suggesting that despite these threats, the rainforest is still thriving, making option C the most suitable inference.

In the next chapter we'll talk about how to write winning essays.

Chapter 6: The Art of the Essay

Mastering the Essay Section: Structure and Evaluation Criteria

For many students, the essay section of the Catholic high school entrance exams can be daunting. However, understanding the structure and evaluation criteria of the essay can demystify this part of the test and set you up for success. Let's explore what you need to know to excel in the essay section.

Essay Structure

1. Introduction: This is where you grab the reader's attention and introduce your thesis statement - the main idea or argument of your essay. Keep it concise and compelling.
2. Body Paragraphs: Typically, you'll have 2-3 body paragraphs. Each should focus on a single point that supports your thesis. Start with a topic sentence, provide evidence or examples, and then a sentence that ties back to your thesis.
3. Conclusion: Summarize your main points and restate your thesis in a new light. This is your last chance to make an impact, so conclude with strength and clarity.

Evaluation Criteria

When grading essays, examiners typically look for several key elements:

1. Thesis and Focus: Is there a clear thesis? Does the essay stay focused on this thesis throughout?
2. Organization and Structure: Is the essay well-organized with a clear introduction, body, and conclusion? Are transitions smooth?
3. Support and Development: Are the points well-supported with evidence or examples? Are ideas developed logically?
4. Grammar and Syntax: Is the essay grammatically correct? Are sentences varied in structure and length?
5. Style and Voice: Does the essay have a consistent and appropriate voice? Is the writing style engaging?
6. Clarity and Precision: Are the ideas clearly expressed? Is the language precise and appropriate for the topic?

Dissecting Successful Essays: Key Points Illustrated

To truly grasp what makes an essay stand out, it's beneficial to analyze successful examples. In this section, we'll dissect a couple of high-scoring essays from past Catholic high school entrance exams to highlight key points that made them successful. Through these analyses, you'll gain insights into effective essay writing techniques.

Example 1: A Persuasive Essay

Topic: "Should students have a say in their curriculum?"

Key Points of Analysis:

1. Strong Thesis Statement: The essay opens with a clear stance: "Students should have a significant say in their curriculum as it enhances learning engagement and prepares them for future responsibilities."
2. Organized Arguments: Each body paragraph presents a well-structured argument supporting the thesis, complete with real-world examples and logical reasoning.
3. Effective Use of Language: The writer uses persuasive language, maintaining a formal but accessible tone, which adds to the essay's persuasive quality.
4. Convincing Conclusion: The conclusion effectively summarizes the key arguments and restates the thesis, reinforcing the writer's position.

Example 2: An Expository Essay

Topic: "Explain the impact of technology on education."

Key Points of Analysis:

1. Clear Exposition: The essay begins with a concise explanation of the role of technology in modern education.
2. Well-Structured Body: Each paragraph tackles a different aspect of technology in education, such as accessibility, personalized learning, and digital literacy.
3. Use of Evidence: The writer incorporates statistics and studies to lend credibility to their explanations.
4. Balanced Perspective: The essay addresses both the positive and negative impacts, demonstrating a well-rounded understanding of the topic.
5. Coherent Conclusion: The conclusion ties together the main points, emphasizing the pervasive impact of technology in educational settings.

Crafting Your Masterpiece: Writing Prompts and Essay Framework

A strong essay is a product of thoughtful planning and structured writing. In this section, we provide you with writing prompts to spark your creativity and a framework to structure your essay effectively. Whether you're crafting a persuasive, narrative, expository, or descriptive essay, these tools will guide you in creating a compelling and coherent piece.

Writing Prompts to Get You Started

1. Persuasive: "Is technology more of a boon or a bane in education?"
2. Narrative: "Write about a time when you overcame a significant challenge."
3. Expository: "Explain the importance of environmental conservation."
4. Descriptive: "Describe your ideal learning environment and why it appeals to you."

Essay Framework

1. Planning:
   - Brainstorm: Jot down ideas, arguments, and examples related to the prompt.
   - Thesis Statement: Develop a clear thesis statement that sets the tone and direction of your essay.
   - Outline: Create an outline to organize your thoughts logically.

2. Introduction:
   - Hook: Start with an engaging sentence to draw the reader in.
   - Background: Provide any necessary background information.
   - Thesis: Present your thesis statement clearly.

3. Body Paragraphs:
   - Topic Sentence: Start each paragraph with a topic sentence that introduces the main idea.
   - Supporting Details: Add arguments, examples, facts, or quotes to support your main idea.
   - Transition: Use transition words or phrases to maintain the flow between paragraphs.

4. Conclusion:
   - Restate Thesis: Begin by restating your thesis in a new light.
   - Summarize Key Points: Briefly recap the main points of your essay.
   - Closing Thought: End with a final thought or call to action that leaves a lasting impression on the reader.

Additional Tips

- Be Concise: Stay on topic and avoid unnecessary wordiness.
- Use Varied Sentence Structure: This keeps the essay interesting and dynamic.

- Proofread: Check for grammar, spelling, and punctuation errors.

In the next chapter we'll talk about the optimal mindset for taking tests.

Chapter 7: Test Psychology and Timing

Staying Focused and Calm: Psychological Strategies for Exam Success

Exams are as much a test of your mental endurance as they are of your academic knowledge. In this section of "Conquering Catholic High School Entrance Exams," we delve into psychological strategies to help you maintain focus and calm during the exam. These techniques are designed to optimize your mental state, enabling you to perform at your best.

Mindfulness and Mental Preparation

1. Visualization: Before the exam, visualize yourself successfully completing the test. Imagine yourself answering questions confidently and calmly.
2. Mindfulness: Practice mindfulness to stay present and focused. Techniques like deep breathing can help center your mind and reduce anxiety.

Stress Management Techniques

1. Breathing Exercises: Use deep, slow breaths to calm your nervous system. Try the 4-7-8 technique: inhale for 4 seconds, hold for 7 seconds, and exhale for 8 seconds.
2. Positive Affirmations: Remind yourself of your preparation and ability. Positive affirmations can boost confidence and reduce negative thoughts.

Staying Focused During the Exam

1. Break the Exam into Segments: Instead of thinking about the exam as a whole, focus on one question or section at a time. This reduces overwhelm and keeps you focused.
2. Regular Mini-Breaks: Every 20-30 minutes, pause briefly to close your eyes, breathe, and refocus. This can prevent mental fatigue.

Managing Test Anxiety

1. Recognize and Reframe: Acknowledge anxious thoughts and reframe them. For instance, change "I might fail" to "I am prepared and will do my best."
2. Stay Grounded: If you feel overwhelmed, ground yourself by focusing on your senses. What can you see, hear, or feel right now?

Time Management

1. Pacing Yourself: Be aware of the time, but don't obsess over it. Allocate time to each section or question and try to stick to this allocation.
2. Avoid Getting Stuck: If a question is too difficult, move on and return to it later if time permits.

Mastering Timing Techniques to Complete Every Section

One of the key challenges in Catholic high school entrance exams is managing time effectively. This section is dedicated to teaching you timing techniques that will ensure you complete all sections of the exam efficiently and without undue stress. Let's explore these strategies to enhance your time management skills during the test.

Understand the Test Format and Time Allocation

1. Know the Format: Familiarize yourself with the structure of the exam – how many sections it has, the type of questions in each section, and the total time allotted.
2. Allocate Time Per Section: Based on the format, allocate a specific amount of time to each section. Consider the number of questions and the difficulty level when doing this.

Practice with Timers

1. Use Timers During Practice: Incorporate timers in your practice sessions. This will help you get a realistic feel for the time pressure and train you to pace yourself.
2. Simulate Exam Conditions: Occasionally, take full-length practice tests under timed conditions to simulate the actual exam scenario.

Efficient Reading and Answering Techniques

1. Skim and Scan: Learn to quickly skim and scan through questions and passages to grasp essential information without wasting time.
2. Answer Easier Questions First: Tackle questions you find easier first. This not only boosts confidence but also ensures you bag those points early on.

Monitor and Adjust

1. Regular Check-ins: During the exam, periodically check the time to see if you are on track. This helps you adjust your pace as needed.
2. Plan for Review Time: Aim to complete each section with some time to spare for review. Even a few minutes to revisit answers can be valuable.

Handling Difficult Questions

1. Decide Quickly: If a question seems too difficult, decide quickly whether to attempt it or move on. Don't spend too much time on any single question.
2. Return if Time Permits: If you have spare time after completing all sections, return to the difficult questions.

Mental Preparation for Timing

1. Stay Calm: If you find yourself running short on time, stay calm. Panic can slow you down. Take a deep breath and focus on answering as efficiently as possible.
2. Accept Imperfection: It's okay if you don't know every answer. Focus on doing your best within the time limits.

Conquering Test Anxiety and Fostering a Positive Mindset

Test anxiety is a common hurdle for many students facing entrance exams. This section focuses on effective methods to overcome this anxiety and maintain a positive mindset, crucial for performing your best during the exam.

Understanding and Acknowledging Test Anxiety

1. Recognize the Symptoms: Be aware of signs like nervousness, rapid heartbeat, or negative thoughts. Recognizing these symptoms is the first step in managing them.
2. Acknowledge Your Feelings: Understand that it's normal to feel anxious about an important test. Accepting your feelings can help reduce their intensity.

Preparation as the Foundation

1. Comprehensive Preparation: Being well-prepared is the most effective way to reduce test anxiety. Confidence in your knowledge can significantly alleviate stress.
2. Practice under Exam Conditions: Regular practice in a timed, exam-like environment can make the actual test feel more familiar and less intimidating.

Techniques to Alleviate Anxiety

1. Breathing Exercises: Use deep breathing techniques to calm your nervous system. Practice these regularly, not just during the test.
2. Positive Visualization: Visualize a successful exam experience. Imagine walking into the test center, feeling confident, and successfully completing the exam.
3. Affirmations: Use positive affirmations to build a positive mindset. Phrases like "I am prepared and capable" can be powerful.

Maintaining a Positive Mindset

1. Focus on Your Efforts: Concentrate on the effort you have put into preparing, rather than the outcome of the test.
2. Self-Care: Ensure you get enough sleep, eat healthily, and engage in activities that relax you in the days leading up to the exam.
3. Avoid Negative Talk: Steer clear of negative conversations about the exam. Surround yourself with positivity.

During the Exam

1. Stay Present: If anxiety arises during the exam, bring yourself back to the present moment. Focus on the question at hand, not the entire exam.
2. Break it Down: Take the exam one question at a time. Avoid overwhelming yourself by thinking about the entire test.
3. Positive Reinforcement: Remind yourself of your preparation and ability. A quick, positive thought can be a powerful tool in managing anxiety.

In the next chapter we'll talk about how your family can help.

Chapter 8: The Family Team

Empowering Parents in Supporting Their Child's Exam Preparation

The role of parents in a student's journey to conquer Catholic high school entrance exams is invaluable. In this section, we offer practical guidance for parents on how to effectively support their child's preparation efforts. By being a part of the 'family team,' parents can significantly contribute to their child's success.

Creating a Supportive Environment

1. Establish a Study Space: Help create a quiet, organized, and dedicated study area free from distractions.
2. Encourage a Routine: Support your child in establishing a consistent study schedule, which can include set times for study, breaks, and relaxation.

Emotional Support and Encouragement

1. Provide Reassurance: Offer encouragement and reassure your child that their best effort is what matters most.
2. Listen and Empathize: Be a sounding board for any concerns or stress your child may be experiencing. Sometimes, simply listening can make a huge difference.

Involvement in the Study Process

1. Understand the Exam: Familiarize yourself with the exam format and content so you can better understand what your child is facing.
2. Review Progress Together: Regularly check in with your child about their progress and any challenges they are facing.

Practical Support

1. Resources and Materials: Ensure your child has access to the necessary study materials, including books, practice tests, and online resources.
2. Healthy Lifestyle: Encourage healthy eating habits, regular exercise, and adequate sleep, all of which are crucial for optimal brain function and stress management.

Encouraging Balance

1. Encourage Breaks and Downtime: Make sure your child takes regular breaks to recharge and encourages participation in leisure activities they enjoy.
2. Family Activities: Engage in relaxing family activities that can provide a break from studying and reduce stress.

Setting Realistic Expectations

1. Focus on Effort, Not Outcome: Emphasize the importance of effort and learning rather than just the outcome of the exam.
2. Avoid Excessive Pressure: Be mindful of the pressure your expectations can place on your child. Encourage them, but also let them know that their worth is not defined by an exam score.

Strengthening Learning Through Communication and Joint Activities

Family involvement can significantly reinforce a student's learning process. This section provides strategies for effective communication and suggests joint activities that families can engage in to support and reinforce learning for Catholic high school entrance exams.

Effective Communication Strategies

1. Regular Check-ins: Establish a routine for regular, informal check-ins. Ask open-ended questions about what they're studying and any challenges they're facing.
2. Active Listening: Show genuine interest in their responses. Active listening involves giving full attention, acknowledging their feelings, and responding thoughtfully.
3. Encourage Self-Expression: Create a safe space for your child to express their thoughts and feelings about the exam preparation. This can help alleviate stress and build confidence.

Joint Learning Activities

1. Study Together: Occasionally, sit down with your child to review what they are learning. This can be as

simple as asking them to teach you a concept they've learned.

2. Educational Games: Engage in educational games or quizzes that relate to exam content. This can make learning fun and interactive.

3. Reading Together: If there are reading materials relevant to their exams, consider setting aside time to read and discuss these together. This not only aids in comprehension but also fosters family bonding.

Encouraging Application of Knowledge

1. Real-World Learning: Encourage your child to apply their knowledge in real-world contexts. For example, if they are learning percentages, involve them in calculating discounts while shopping.

2. Project-Based Activities: Engage in small projects that relate to their study material. For instance, if they are studying history, you might visit a museum or historical site together.

Building a Supportive Learning Environment

1. Discuss Learning Techniques: Talk about different study methods and which ones seem to work best for your child, reinforcing the idea that everyone learns differently.

2. Celebrate Efforts: Acknowledge and celebrate the effort they put into studying, regardless of the

outcomes. This can be as simple as a family dinner to recognize their hard work.

Navigating Stress Management in Exam Preparation

The journey towards Catholic high school entrance exams can be a stressful time for students. In this section, we discuss the crucial role of stress management in the preparation process. Effective stress management not only supports academic success but also contributes to the overall well-being of the student.

Understanding Stress in the Context of Exam Prep

1. Recognize the Signs: Be aware of signs of stress in your child, such as changes in sleep patterns, irritability, or a decline in academic performance.
2. Normalize Stress: Help your child understand that feeling stressed is a normal response to challenging situations like exams.

Strategies for Managing Stress

1. Encourage Open Communication: Create an environment where your child feels comfortable discussing their anxieties and pressures.
2. Balanced Lifestyle: Encourage a balanced lifestyle that includes physical activities, hobbies, and social interactions alongside study commitments.

Family's Role in Stress Management

1. Be a Source of Calm: Maintain a calm and positive home environment. Your own response to stress can significantly influence your child.
2. Support, Don't Pressure: Be supportive of their efforts rather than adding pressure. Emphasize effort and learning over grades and outcomes.

Practical Stress-Relief Techniques

1. Relaxation Techniques: Teach your child simple relaxation techniques such as deep breathing, meditation, or yoga.
2. Healthy Routine: Encourage a healthy routine that includes regular exercise, adequate sleep, and nutritious meals.

Time Management as a Stress Reducer

1. Help with Scheduling: Assist your child in creating a realistic study schedule that includes breaks and leisure time.

2. Set Realistic Goals: Help your child set achievable study goals, which can reduce feelings of being overwhelmed.

Encouraging Perspective

1. Long-Term View: Remind your child that while important, these exams are just one part of their educational journey.
2. Positive Reinforcement: Regularly reinforce that you are proud of their efforts and that their value is not determined by exam results.

In the next chapter we'll talk about what you need to think about beyond the test.

Chapter 9: Beyond the Test

Understanding the Broader Application Process for Catholic High Schools

While excelling in entrance exams is a significant milestone, it's just one part of the broader application process for Catholic high schools. This section offers insights into the various components of the application process, helping you navigate this journey with confidence and clarity.

Overview of the Application Process

1. Academic Records: Your child's academic records, including grades and teacher recommendations, play a vital role. Maintain a strong academic performance throughout middle school.
2. Application Forms: Complete all required forms accurately and submit them before deadlines. Pay attention to details and ensure that all information is correct.

Personal Statements and Essays

1. Reflect Personality and Values: Personal statements and essays are opportunities for your child to express their personality, aspirations, and values. Encourage them to be authentic and reflective in their writing.
2. Demonstrate Fit: Use these written components to demonstrate how your child aligns with the school's ethos and values.

Extracurricular Activities and Community Involvement

1. Showcase a Well-Rounded Profile: Participation in extracurricular activities and community service

projects can illustrate your child's well-roundedness and commitment to community values.
2. Highlight Leadership and Initiative: Leadership roles or initiatives in projects can be especially impactful, showcasing responsibility and leadership qualities.

Interviews

1. Preparation is Key: If the application process includes an interview, help your child prepare by conducting mock interviews.
2. Communication Skills: Focus on developing strong communication skills, including clear articulation of thoughts and active listening.

Recommendations

1. Choose Wisely: Select recommenders who know your child well and can speak to their strengths, character, and suitability for the school.
2. Request Early: Give recommenders ample time to write thoughtful recommendations.

The Importance of Fit

1. Research Schools: Understand each school's culture, values, and programs. This helps in tailoring applications and choosing schools that are a good fit for your child.

2. Align Interests and Goals: Consider how each school aligns with your child's interests and long-term goals.

Managing Expectations

1. Stay Positive but Realistic: Encourage optimism while also preparing for any outcome. The process can be competitive, and it's important to have a balanced perspective.
2. Backup Plans: Have a list of alternative schools and understand their application processes as well.

The Vital Role of Extracurricular Activities and Personal Statements

In the journey to Catholic high school admission, extracurricular activities and personal statements play crucial roles that extend beyond academic performance. This section emphasizes the importance of these components in the application process, providing actionable advice to make the most of these opportunities.

Extracurricular Activities: More Than Just Hobbies

Extracurricular activities are a window into a student's interests, passions, and character. They demonstrate to admissions committees how students might contribute to the school community beyond academics.

1. Diverse Interests: Encourage participation in a variety of activities, including sports, arts, clubs, and community service. This diversity shows adaptability and a willingness to explore new areas.
2. Leadership and Teamwork: Roles that demonstrate leadership or teamwork are particularly valuable, as they highlight skills like responsibility, cooperation, and the ability to motivate others.
3. Commitment and Growth: Long-term commitment to an activity is more impressive than short stints in many. It shows dedication and the ability to grow and improve in a chosen area.

Personal Statements: A Narrative of Self

Personal statements are a unique opportunity for students to speak directly to admissions committees. They provide a narrative of who the student is, their aspirations, and why they are a good fit for the school.

1. Authentic Voice: Encourage your child to write in their own voice, expressing genuine thoughts and

feelings. Authenticity resonates more than trying to fit a perceived ideal.

2. Reflective and Insightful: Good personal statements reflect introspection and insight. Discuss experiences that shaped their personality, values, or goals.

3. Relevance to the School: Tailor the statement to reflect how your child's values and goals align with the school's ethos. Researching the school's mission and values can provide useful insights for this alignment.

4. Clear and Concise: While being reflective and insightful, it's also important to be clear and concise. Adhere to word limits and focus on presenting thoughts in a coherent manner.

Bridging Activities and Statements

1. Linking Experiences: Use extracurricular experiences as examples or narratives in the personal statement to illustrate personal qualities or growth.

2. Showcasing Versatility: Highlight how diverse interests have contributed to a well-rounded personality and a broad perspective.

Excelling in Interviews and Supplementary Essays

The interview and supplementary essays are integral parts of the Catholic high school application process. They provide opportunities to showcase your personality, intellect, and suitability for the school. This section offers practical tips to excel in both areas.

Preparing for Interviews

1. Research the School: Understanding the school's values, programs, and ethos can help you answer questions in a way that aligns with their expectations.
2. Practice Common Questions: Prepare for questions like "Why do you want to attend this school?" or "What are your academic and personal strengths?" Practice articulating clear, honest, and concise responses.
3. Mock Interviews: Conduct mock interviews with a family member, teacher, or mentor. This practice can ease nerves and improve your confidence.
4. Non-Verbal Communication: Pay attention to non-verbal cues like eye contact, handshakes, and posture. These are just as important as your verbal responses.
5. Prepare Questions: Have a couple of questions ready to ask the interviewer. This shows your interest in the school and that you've done your homework.

Writing Supplementary Essays

1. Read Instructions Carefully: Understand the essay prompt and adhere strictly to any word limits and formatting guidelines.
2. Personalize Your Response: Tailor your essay to reflect how you align with the specific school's values and how you can contribute to their community.
3. Be Specific and Reflective: Avoid generic statements. Use specific examples from your life to illustrate your points and reflect on what you learned from these experiences.
4. Show Don't Tell: Use descriptive language to 'show' the reader your qualities and experiences, rather than just 'telling' them.
5. Proofread and Revise: Ensure your essays are free from grammatical errors and typos. Have a teacher, mentor, or parent review your essays for feedback.

Both the interview and supplementary essays are platforms to communicate what makes you the ideal candidate for the school. By preparing thoroughly and presenting yourself authentically, you can make a lasting impression that goes beyond your test scores.

Embrace these opportunities to let your personality, aspirations, and thoughtfulness shine through. This is your moment to make a personal connection with the school.*

In the next chapter we'll talk about your game plan for exam day.

Chapter 10: Exam Day Game Plan

A Strategic Approach to the Days Leading Up to and Including the Exam Day

The final days leading up to the exam and the exam day itself are critical periods. A well-planned approach during this time can significantly enhance your performance. This section offers a detailed plan to ensure you are mentally and physically prepared for the big day.

The Week Before the Exam

1. Review, Don't Cram: Focus on reviewing key concepts rather than trying to learn new material. This helps reinforce what you already know.
2. Practice Tests: Take a couple of practice tests early in the week for last-minute assessments of your understanding.

3. Relaxation Techniques: Incorporate relaxation techniques into your daily routine to manage stress, such as deep breathing, meditation, or light exercise.

The Night Before the Exam

1. Gather Necessary Materials: Prepare everything you need for the exam, including admission tickets, identification, pens, pencils, a calculator (if allowed), and a watch.
2. Early Night: Ensure you get a good night's sleep. Aim for at least 8 hours to wake up refreshed.
3. Relaxing Evening: Engage in a relaxing activity to calm your nerves, like reading a book or listening to soothing music.

Exam Day Morning

1. Healthy Breakfast: Eat a nutritious breakfast that will provide sustained energy. Avoid overly sugary foods that can cause a mid-exam energy crash.
2. Arrive Early: Aim to arrive at the exam center at least 30 minutes early to avoid any last-minute rush and to settle in.

During the Exam

1. Read Instructions Carefully: Take a few minutes to read all instructions thoroughly to avoid any misunderstandings.

2. Time Management: Allocate your time wisely across sections, and keep an eye on the clock without obsessing over it.

3. Stay Calm and Focused: If you feel anxious, take deep breaths to regain focus. Approach each question methodically.

After the Exam

1. Post-Exam Review: Resist the urge to immediately discuss the exam with peers, as it can lead to unnecessary stress.

2. Relax and Recharge: Engage in a relaxing activity post-exam to decompress and reward yourself for your hard work.

Essential Checklist and Mental Preparation for the Big Day

Approaching exam day with a clear plan and the right mindset can greatly influence your performance. This section provides a checklist of items to bring to the testing center and tips for mental preparation, ensuring you're fully equipped and mentally ready for the exam.

Checklist for the Testing Center

1. Admission Ticket: Bring your exam admission ticket, as it's required for entry.
2. Valid Identification: Carry a valid ID with your photograph and name.
3. Writing Implements: Pack several pens and pencils, and if allowed, an eraser and sharpener.
4. Approved Calculator: If calculators are permitted for your exam, ensure it's an approved model.
5. Watch or Timer: Bring a watch or a small timer to manage your time, ensuring it doesn't make noise.
6. Snacks and Water: Pack light snacks and water for breaks, focusing on items that won't cause distractions or mess.
7. Extra Layers: Consider an extra sweater or jacket in case the testing room is cooler than expected.

Mental Preparation Tips

1. Positive Visualization: Spend a few minutes visualizing a successful exam experience. Imagine walking into the testing center, feeling confident, and efficiently working through the questions.
2. Affirmations: Use positive affirmations to boost your confidence. Phrases like "I am prepared and capable" can help maintain a positive mindset.
3. Mindful Breathing: If you feel anxious, practice mindful breathing. Focus on taking slow, deep breaths to calm your nerves.

4. Stay Present: Concentrate on the current moment rather than worrying about the entire exam. Tackle one question at a time.

5. Avoid Negative Talk: Steer clear of negative discussions with peers before the exam as they can increase anxiety.

6. Rest and Relaxation: Ensure you get a good night's sleep before the exam day. A well-rested mind is more alert and focused.

With this checklist and mental preparation tips, you are set to approach your exam day with everything you need, both physically and mentally. Remember, your preparation goes beyond studying – it's about being ready in every aspect.

Enter the exam hall with confidence, knowing you are fully prepared for the task ahead. This is your moment to shine!*

Section-by-Section Strategies for Maximizing Exam Performance

Tackling an entrance exam requires a strategic approach for each section. This part of the chapter focuses on specific strategies for different sections of the Catholic high school entrance exams, ensuring you can effectively navigate through the test and optimize your performance.

Verbal Skills Section

1. Skim and Scan: Quickly skim through the questions first, then scan the passage for relevant information. This helps in efficiently finding answers.
2. Vocabulary in Context: For vocabulary questions, look at how the word is used in the sentence or passage to determine its meaning.
3. Grammar and Syntax: Pay close attention to sentence structure and grammar. Errors can often be spotted by reading the sentence out loud in your head.

Mathematics Section

1. Review First: Glance through the questions to identify those you feel confident about. Tackle these first to secure quick points.
2. Estimation and Elimination: Use estimation to quickly eliminate implausible answers, especially in multiple-choice questions.
3. Show Your Work: Even if it's a rough calculation, write it down. This can help keep track of your thought process and make it easier to review if you have time left over.

Reading Comprehension Section

1. Prioritize Passages: Quickly assess the passages and start with the ones that seem most straightforward.
2. Active Reading: Engage with the passage as you read, making mental or physical notes of key points.
3. Question Keywords: Look for keywords in questions that will guide you back to relevant parts of the passage.

Essay Section (If Applicable)

1. Plan Before Writing: Spend a few minutes planning your essay. Jot down your thesis statement and key points.
2. Structured Response: Ensure your essay has a clear introduction, body, and conclusion. Stick to the structure to maintain coherence.
3. Proofread: If time allows, quickly review your essay for any grammatical errors or typos.

Approaching each section with these strategies in mind can greatly enhance your ability to navigate the exam efficiently and effectively. Remember, the key is to stay calm, focused, and methodical in your approach to every part of the exam.

Go into each section with a plan, execute it with confidence, and you'll maximize your chances of success.

Practice Exams

Section Breakdown and Question Types

The HSPT typically consists of five sections: Verbal Skills, Quantitative Skills, Reading Comprehension, Mathematics, and Language Skills.

Your practice exam should include a mix of question types found in each of these sections.

1. Verbal Skills (60 questions):
   - Synonyms and Antonyms: Test understanding of word meanings.
   - Analogies: Assess the ability to discern relationships between words.
   - Logic: Evaluate logical reasoning skills.
2. Quantitative Skills (52 questions):
   - Number Series: Analyze sequences of numbers.

- Geometric Comparisons: Assess understanding of basic geometric concepts.
- Non-Verbal Reasoning: Evaluate the ability to understand and analyze visual information.

3. Reading Comprehension (62 questions):
   - Passage Analysis: Include passages followed by questions testing comprehension.
   - Main Idea, Details, Inference: Questions should assess the ability to find the main idea, details, and make inferences.

4. Mathematics (64 questions):
   - Arithmetic: Include questions on basic operations.
   - Basic Algebra: Test understanding of simple equations and concepts.
   - Geometry: Assess knowledge of basic geometric principles and problems.

5. Language Skills (60 questions):
   - Grammar and Punctuation: Include questions testing knowledge of grammar rules.
   - Sentence Structure: Evaluate the ability to understand and correct sentence structure.
   - Spelling and Capitalization: Test spelling and the use of capital letters.

Section1: Verbal Skills

Question 1: Synonyms

Prompt: Choose the word that is most nearly similar in meaning to the word provided: "Diminish"

A) Increase
B) Reduce
C) Brighten

D) Expand

Answer: B) Reduce

Explanation: 'Diminish' means to make or become less. The word that best matches this meaning is 'reduce', which also means to make something smaller or less in size, amount, or degree.

Question 2: Analogies

Prompt: Bread is to Bake as Ice is to:

A) Melt
B) Freeze

C) Cut

D) Water

Answer: A) Melt

Explanation: This question is based on a relationship of transformation. Bread is transformed by baking, just as ice is transformed by melting. Therefore, the correct answer is 'melt', which signifies the transformation of ice.

Question 3: Logic

Prompt: If all Zips are Zaps and some Zaps are Zops, which of the following must be true?

A) All Zips are Zops
B) Some Zips are Zops
C) No Zips are Zops

D) Cannot be determined from the information given

Answer: D) Cannot be determined from the information given

Explanation: From the statements given, we know that Zips are a subset of Zaps, and some Zaps (but not necessarily all) are Zops. Therefore, it is possible but not certain that some Zips are Zops. Since there is no definitive connection between Zips and Zops based

on the information provided, the correct answer is
'Cannot be determined from the information given'.

Question 4: Synonyms

Prompt: Choose the word that is most nearly similar
in meaning to "Enigmatic":

A) Clear
B) Puzzling
C) Obvious

D) Simple

Answer: B) Puzzling

Explanation: 'Enigmatic' refers to something that is
mysterious or difficult to understand. The word
'puzzling' closely matches this meaning, as it also
implies something that is confusing or not easily
understood.

Question 5: Analogies

Prompt: Night is to Darkness as Day is to:

A) Sun
B) Light
C) Morning

D) Noon

Answer: B) Light

Explanation: This analogy is based on inherent characteristics. Night is characterized by darkness, just as day is characterized by light. Therefore, 'Light' is the correct answer.

Question 6: Logic

Prompt: If no Kites are Bikes and all Bikes are Rides, which is true?

A) Some Kites are Rides
B) No Kites are Rides
C) All Kites are Rides

D) Cannot be determined from the information given

Answer: D) Cannot be determined from the information given

Explanation: While we know that all Bikes are Rides, there's no direct relationship established between Kites and Rides. Therefore, the relationship between Kites and Rides cannot be determined from the given information.

Question 7: Synonyms

Prompt: The word "Obsolete" most nearly means:

A) Modern
B) Outdated
C) Useful

D) New

Answer: B) Outdated

Explanation: 'Obsolete' refers to something that is no longer in use or out of date. The synonym that best matches this meaning is 'outdated'.

Question 8: Analogies

Prompt: Pen is to Write as Knife is to:

A) Cut
B) Sharp
C) Stab

D) Metal

Answer: A) Cut

Explanation: This analogy is based on function. A pen is used to write, just as a knife is used to cut. Therefore, 'Cut' is the correct answer.

Question 9: Logic

Prompt: If some Pines are Trees and all Trees are Plants, which is true?

A) All Pines are Plants
B) Some Pines are not Plants
C) No Pines are Plants

D) Some Pines are Plants

Answer: D) Some Pines are Plants

Explanation: Since some Pines are Trees and all Trees are Plants, it follows that some Pines must be Plants. Therefore, 'Some Pines are Plants' is the correct answer.

Question 10: Synonyms

Prompt: The word "Vivacious" most nearly means:

A) Energetic
B) Dull
C) Tired

D) Slow

Answer: A) Energetic

Explanation: 'Vivacious' describes someone lively and spirited, which is closely synonymous with 'energetic'.

Question 11: Synonyms

Prompt: Choose the word that most closely matches the meaning of "Candid":

A) Evasive
B) Honest
C) Secretive

D) Rude

Answer: B) Honest

Explanation: 'Candid' refers to being truthful and straightforward. The synonym that best aligns with this meaning is 'honest'.

Question 12: Analogies

Prompt: Tree is to Leaf as Book is to:

A) Library
B) Page
C) Author

D) Cover

Answer: B) Page

Explanation: This analogy is based on a part-to-whole relationship. A leaf is a part of a tree, just as a page is a part of a book. Therefore, 'Page' is the correct answer.

Question 13: Logic

Prompt: If all Mints are Herbs and no Herbs are Trees, then:

A) All Mints are Trees
B) Some Mints are Trees
C) No Mints are Trees

D) Cannot be determined from the information given

Answer: C) No Mints are Trees

Explanation: Since all Mints are Herbs and no Herbs are Trees, it logically follows that no Mints can be Trees. Hence, 'No Mints are Trees' is the correct answer.

Question 14: Synonyms

Prompt: Choose the word that most closely matches the meaning of "Lucid":

A) Obscure
B) Clear

C) Complex

D) Ambiguous

Answer: B) Clear

Explanation: 'Lucid' means easy to understand or clear. The synonym that best aligns with this meaning is 'clear'.

Question 15: Analogies

Prompt: Painter is to Canvas as Writer is to:

A) Book
B) Pen
C) Paper

D) Story

Answer: C) Paper

Explanation: This analogy is based on the medium used for work. A painter works on a canvas, and a writer works on paper. Thus, 'Paper' is the correct answer.

Question 16: Logic

Prompt: If all Roses are Flowers and some Flowers are Red, then:

A) All Roses are Red
B) Some Roses are Red
C) No Roses are Red

D) Cannot be determined from the information given

Answer: D) Cannot be determined from the information given

Explanation: While all roses are flowers, the information that some flowers are red doesn't necessarily apply to all roses. Therefore, the relationship between roses and the color red cannot be determined from the given information.

Question 17: Synonyms

Prompt: The word "Ingenious" most nearly means:

A) Simple
B) Clever
C) Naive

D) Slow

Answer: B) Clever

Explanation: 'Ingenious' refers to something clever, original, and inventive. The synonym that best matches this meaning is 'clever'.

Question 18: Analogies

Prompt: Fish is to Swim as Bird is to:

A) Nest
B) Fly
C) Sing

D) Feather

Answer: B) Fly

Explanation: This analogy is based on the action typically associated with each creature. Fish swim, and birds fly. Therefore, 'Fly' is the correct answer.

Question 19: Logic

Prompt: If all Gliders are Planes and no Planes are Jets, then:

A) All Gliders are Jets
B) Some Gliders are Jets
C) No Gliders are Jets

D) Cannot be determined from the information given

Answer: C) No Gliders are Jets

Explanation: Since all Gliders are categorized as Planes, and no Planes are Jets, it logically follows that no Gliders can be Jets. Thus, 'No Gliders are Jets' is the correct answer.

Question 20: Synonyms

Prompt: The word "Benevolent" most nearly means:

A) Malevolent
B) Kind
C) Indifferent

D) Harsh

Answer: B) Kind

Explanation: 'Benevolent' means well-meaning and kindly. The synonym that best matches this meaning is 'kind'.

Question 21: Synonyms

Prompt: Choose the word that most closely matches the meaning of "Prodigious":

A) Small
B) Ordinary
C) Enormous

D) Weak

Answer: C) Enormous

Explanation: 'Prodigious' means remarkably or impressively great in size, extent, or degree. The word 'enormous' is a synonym that captures this meaning.

Question 22: Analogies

Prompt: Cold is to Ice as Heat is to:

A) Sun
B) Fire
C) Light

D) Summer

Answer: B) Fire

Explanation: This analogy is based on causation. Cold is associated with ice as heat is associated with fire. Fire is a source of heat, just as ice is a form of cold.

Question 23: Logic

Prompt: If some Sprints are Runs and all Runs are Races, then:

A) All Sprints are Races
B) Some Sprints are Races
C) No Sprints are Races

D) Cannot be determined from the information given

Answer: B) Some Sprints are Races

Explanation: Since some Sprints are categorized as Runs, and all Runs are categorized as Races, it logically follows that some Sprints must be Races. Thus, 'Some Sprints are Races' is the correct answer.

Question 24: Synonyms

Prompt: The word "Convoluted" most nearly means:

A) Straightforward
B) Complicated
C) Narrow

D) Smooth

Answer: B) Complicated

Explanation: 'Convoluted' refers to something that is extremely complex and difficult to follow. The synonym that best matches this meaning is 'complicated'.

Question 25: Analogies

Prompt: Pen is to Write as Brush is to:

A) Paint

B) Clean
C) Comb

D) Stroke

Answer: A) Paint

Explanation: This analogy is based on the function or purpose of the objects. A pen is used to write, and a brush is used to paint. Therefore, 'Paint' is the correct answer.

Certainly! Here are eight more sample questions for the Verbal Skills section of the HSPT, along with answers and detailed explanations for each. These questions cover a range of types including synonyms, analogies, and logical reasoning.

Question 26: Synonyms

Prompt: Identify the synonym for "Immutable":

  A) Changeable
  B) Constant
  C) Flexible
  D) Variable

Answer: B) Constant

Explanation: 'Immutable' means unchanging over time or unable to be changed. The word 'constant' shares this meaning, making it the correct synonym.

Question 27: Analogies

Prompt: Water is to Thirst as Food is to:

A) Eat
B) Hunger
C) Cooking
D) Plate

Answer: B) Hunger

Explanation: This analogy is based on a cause and effect relationship. Water satisfies thirst just as food satisfies hunger. Thus, 'Hunger' is the correct answer.

Question 28: Logic

Prompt: If all Tulips are Flowers and some Flowers are Fragrant, then:

A) All Tulips are Fragrant
B) Some Tulips are Fragrant
C) No Tulips are Fragrant

D) Cannot be determined from the information given

Answer: D) Cannot be determined from the information given

Explanation: Since only 'some' Flowers are Fragrant and all Tulips are Flowers, there's no definitive way to conclude the relationship between Tulips and being Fragrant. Therefore, the answer cannot be determined from the given information.

Question 29: Synonyms

Prompt: The best synonym for "Prolific":

A) Scarce
B) Barren
C) Abundant
D) Infrequent

Answer: C) Abundant

Explanation: 'Prolific' means present in large numbers or quantities; plentiful. The word 'abundant' also means existing or available in large quantities; plentiful, making it the correct synonym.

Question 30: Analogies

Prompt: Exciting is to Thrilling as Boring is to:

A) Tedious
B) Interesting
C) Fascinating
D) Stimulating

Answer: A) Tedious

Explanation: 'Exciting' is similar in degree to 'thrilling', just as 'boring' is similar in degree to 'tedious'. Both pairs are synonymous in intensity.

Question 31: Logic

Prompt: If all Novels are Books and no Books are Magazines, then:

A) All Novels are Magazines
B) Some Novels are Magazines
C) No Novels are Magazines
D) Cannot be determined from the information given

Answer: C) No Novels are Magazines

Explanation: If all Novels fall under the category of Books, and no Books are categorized as Magazines, it logically follows that Novels cannot be Magazines. Thus, 'No Novels are Magazines' is the correct answer.

Question 32: Synonyms

Prompt: Choose the word most similar in meaning to "Meticulous":

A) Careless
B) Precise
C) Negligent
D) Hasty

Answer: B) Precise

Explanation: 'Meticulous' means showing great attention to detail; very careful and precise. Therefore, the best synonym is 'precise'.

Question 33: Analogies

Prompt: Owl is to Night as Eagle is to:

A) Sky

B) Day
C) Nest
D) Mountain

Answer: B) Day

Explanation: Owls are known for being active at night, just as eagles are commonly associated with being active during the day. So, 'Day' is the correct answer in this analogy.

Question 34: Synonyms

Prompt: Select the synonym for "Melancholy":

A) Joyful
B) Sad
C) Peaceful
D) Angry

Answer: B) Sad

Explanation: 'Melancholy' refers to a feeling of pensive sadness, typically with no obvious cause. The word 'sad' is synonymous with this feeling.

Question 35: Analogies

Prompt: Snow is to Winter as Sun is to:

A) Rain
B) Summer
C) Cloud
D) Weather

Answer: B) Summer

Explanation: Snow is commonly associated with winter, just as the sun is commonly associated with summer. Therefore, 'Summer' is the correct answer.

Question 36: Logic

Prompt: If all Aardvarks are Animals and no Animals are Plants, then:

A) All Aardvarks are Plants
B) Some Aardvarks are Plants
C) No Aardvarks are Plants
D) Cannot be determined from the information given

Answer: C) No Aardvarks are Plants

Explanation: Given that all Aardvarks are Animals, and no Animals are Plants, it logically follows that

Aardvarks cannot be Plants. Therefore, 'No Aardvarks are Plants' is the correct answer.

Question 37: Synonyms

Prompt: Choose the word that most closely matches the meaning of "Tenacious":

    A) Weak
    B) Fleeting
    C) Persistent
    D) Indifferent

Answer: C) Persistent

Explanation: 'Tenacious' means tending to keep a firm hold of something; clinging or adhering closely. The word 'persistent' captures this sense of determination and perseverance.

Question 38: Analogies

Prompt: Silent is to Loud as Ancient is to:

    A) Historic
    B) Modern
    C) Old

D) Forgotten

Answer: B) Modern

Explanation: The relationship here is opposites. Silent is the opposite of loud, and ancient is the opposite of modern.

Question 39: Logic

Prompt: If some Smartphones are Cameras and all Cameras are Devices, then:

A) All Smartphones are Devices
B) Some Smartphones are Devices
C) No Smartphones are Devices
D) Cannot be determined from the information given

Answer: B) Some Smartphones are Devices

Explanation: Since some Smartphones are Cameras, and all Cameras are Devices, it logically follows that some Smartphones must be Devices. Therefore, 'Some Smartphones are Devices' is the correct answer.

Question 40: Synonyms

Prompt: The best synonym for "Ephemeral":

A) Lasting
B) Fleeting
C) Eternal
D) Perpetual

Answer: B) Fleeting

Explanation: 'Ephemeral' refers to something that lasts for a very short time. 'Fleeting' also means lasting for a very short time, making it the correct synonym.

Question 41: Analogies

Prompt: Author is to Book as Sculptor is to:

A) Stone
B) Museum
C) Statue
D) Tool

Answer: C) Statue

Explanation: An author creates a book, just as a sculptor creates a statue. Therefore, 'Statue' is the correct answer in this analogy.

Practicing with these types of questions will help improve your skills in synonyms, analogies, and logical reasoning, which are essential for performing well in the Verbal Skills section of the HSPT.

Continued practice and familiarity with these question types will be key to your success in this exam section.

Question 42: Synonyms

Prompt: Select the synonym for "Fastidious":

A) Careless
B) Meticulous
C) Rash
D) Hasty

Answer: B) Meticulous

Explanation: 'Fastidious' means very attentive to and concerned about accuracy and detail. 'Meticulous' shares this meaning, making it the correct synonym.

Question 43: Analogies

Prompt: Ice is to Cold as Oven is to:

A) Hot
B) Cook
C) Kitchen
D) Food

Answer: A) Hot

Explanation: Ice is associated with cold, just as an oven is associated with heat. Therefore, 'Hot' is the correct answer, based on the relationship of association.

Question 44: Logic

Prompt: If all Dolphins are Mammals and some Mammals are Large, then:

A) All Dolphins are Large
B) Some Dolphins are Large

C) No Dolphins are Large

D) Cannot be determined from the information given

Answer: D) Cannot be determined from the information given

Explanation: The statement that some mammals are large does not specifically include or exclude dolphins. Therefore, the relationship between dolphins and being large cannot be determined from the given information.

Question 45: Synonyms

Prompt: The word "Covert" most nearly means:

A) Open

B) Hidden

C) Obvious

D) Exposed

Answer: B) Hidden

Explanation: 'Covert' refers to something not openly acknowledged or displayed. 'Hidden' is a synonym that captures this sense of being concealed or secret.

Question 46: Analogies

Prompt: Pen is to Writing as Knife is to:

A) Cutting
B) Cooking
C) Eating
D) Sharpening

Answer: A) Cutting

Explanation: Just as a pen is a tool used for writing, a knife is a tool used for cutting. Hence, 'Cutting' is the correct answer in this analogy.

Question 47: Logic

Prompt: If all Roses are Flowers and no Flowers are Trees, then:

A) All Roses are Trees
B) Some Roses are Trees
C) No Roses are Trees
D) Cannot be determined from the information given

Answer: C) No Roses are Trees

Explanation: Since all Roses are categorized as Flowers, and no Flowers are categorized as Trees, it logically follows that Roses cannot be Trees. Thus, 'No Roses are Trees' is the correct answer.

Question 48: Synonyms

Prompt: Choose the word that most closely matches the meaning of "Capricious":

A) Steady
B) Predictable
C) Whimsical
D) Unchanging

Answer: C) Whimsical

Explanation: 'Capricious' describes a tendency to make sudden and unpredictable changes. 'Whimsical' captures this notion of being subject to whims or unpredictable behavior.

Question 49: Analogies

Prompt: Desert is to Arid as Ocean is to:

A) Wet

B) Salty
C) Deep
D) Blue

Answer: A) Wet

Explanation: 'Arid' is a defining characteristic of a desert, just as 'wet' is a defining characteristic of an ocean. Therefore, 'Wet' is the correct answer, based on the relationship of defining characteristics.

Question 50: Synonyms

Prompt: Identify the synonym for "Arduous":

A) Easy
B) Difficult
C) Pleasant
D) Simple

Answer: B) Difficult

Explanation: 'Arduous' means requiring a lot of effort and hard work. The word 'difficult' is a synonym that captures this meaning.

Question 51: Analogies

Prompt: Drought is to Rain as Famine is to:

A) Food
B) Hunger
C) Crop
D) Farm

Answer: A) Food

Explanation: Drought is a lack of rain, and famine is a lack of food. Thus, 'Food' is the correct answer, as it is the missing element in a famine, just as rain is in a drought.

Question 52: Logic

Prompt: If all Tigers are Cats and no Cats are Birds, then:

A) All Tigers are Birds
B) Some Tigers are Birds
C) No Tigers are Birds
D) Cannot be determined from the information given

Answer: C) No Tigers are Birds

Explanation: Since Tigers fall under the category of Cats, and no Cats are Birds, it logically follows that

Tigers cannot be Birds. Therefore, 'No Tigers are Birds' is the correct answer.

Question 53: Synonyms

Prompt: The word "Lethargic" most nearly means:

A) Energetic
B) Active
C) Sluggish
D) Vigorous

Answer: C) Sluggish

Explanation: 'Lethargic' refers to a state of tiredness or a lack of energy. 'Sluggish' also means slow-moving or lacking energy, making it the correct synonym.

Question 54: Analogies

Prompt: Whisper is to Shout as Stroll is to:

A) Run
B) Wander
C) Skip
D) March

Answer: A) Run

Explanation: Whispering is a quiet form of speaking, and shouting is a loud form. Similarly, strolling is a slow form of walking, and running is a fast form. Therefore, 'Run' is the correct answer.

Question 55: Logic

Prompt: If all Pencils are Writing Instruments and some Writing Instruments are Pens, then:

A) All Pencils are Pens
B) Some Pencils are Pens
C) No Pencils are Pens
D) Cannot be determined from the information given

Answer: D) Cannot be determined from the information given

Explanation: The information that some Writing Instruments are Pens does not specifically include or exclude Pencils. Therefore, the relationship between Pencils and Pens cannot be determined from the given information.

Question 56: Synonyms

Prompt: Choose the word that most closely matches the meaning of "Cordial":

A) Hostile
B) Warm
C) Indifferent
D) Cold

Answer: B) Warm

Explanation: 'Cordial' means warm and friendly. The word 'warm' is a synonym that captures this sense of friendliness and approachability.

Question 57: Analogies

Prompt: Frost is to Cold as Dew is to:

A) Wet
B) Morning
C) Night
D) Grass

Answer: B) Morning

Explanation: Frost forms due to cold temperatures, just as dew typically forms in the morning due to condensation. Thus, 'Morning' is the correct answer, based on the condition of formation.

Question 58: Synonyms

Prompt: Choose the word that most closely matches the meaning of "Ineffable":

A) Expressible
B) Indescribable
C) Noisy
D) Understandable

Answer: B) Indescribable

Explanation: 'Ineffable' refers to something that is too great or extreme to be expressed in words. 'Indescribable' is the synonym that best captures this notion of being beyond description.

Question 59: Analogies

Prompt: Library is to Books as Orchard is to:

A) Leaves
B) Trees
C) Fruit
D) Branches

Answer: C) Fruit

Explanation: A library is a place where books are collected, just as an orchard is a place where fruit is grown and collected. Therefore, 'Fruit' is the correct answer, highlighting the product of each location.

Question 60: Logic

Prompt: If all Roses are Red and some Red things are Cars, then:

A) All Roses are Cars
B) Some Roses are Cars
C) No Roses are Cars
D) Cannot be determined from the information given

Answer: D) Cannot be determined from the information given

Explanation: The fact that some Red things are Cars does not specifically include or exclude Roses. Since there is no direct link established between Roses and

Cars, the relationship between them cannot be determined from the given information.

SECTION 2: Quantitative Skills (52 questions):

Question 1: Number Series

Prompt: What is the next number in the series: 2, 4, 8, 16, ...?

  A) 24
  B) 32
  C) 30
  D) 18

Answer: B) 32

Explanation: This is a series where each number is multiplied by 2 to get the next number. So, 16 x 2 = 32.

Question 2: Geometric Comparisons

Prompt: Which shape has more sides: a pentagon or a hexagon?

  A) Pentagon
  B) Hexagon
  C) Both have the same
  D) Cannot be determined

Answer: B) Hexagon

Explanation: A pentagon has 5 sides, while a hexagon has 6 sides. Therefore, a hexagon has more sides.

Question 3: Non-Verbal Reasoning

Prompt: If a circle represents boys and a square represents swimmers, which shape would represent boys who are swimmers?

  A) A separate circle and square
  B) An overlapping area between the circle and square
  C) A circle inside a square
  D) A square inside a circle

Answer: B) An overlapping area between the circle and square

Explanation: The overlapping area between the circle and square represents individuals who are both boys (circle) and swimmers (square).

Question 4: Number Series

Prompt: Find the missing number: 3, 9, 27, __, 243

    A) 54
    B) 81
    C) 72
    D) 108

Answer: B) 81

Explanation: This series is each number multiplied by 3. So, 27 x 3 = 81.

Question 5: Geometric Comparisons

Prompt: Which has more angles: a triangle or a rectangle?

    A) Triangle
    B) Rectangle
    C) Both have the same
    D) Cannot be determined

Answer: B) Rectangle

Explanation: A triangle has 3 angles, while a rectangle has 4 angles. Therefore, a rectangle has more angles.

Question 6: Non-Verbal Reasoning

Prompt: If a triangle represents cars and a circle represents electric vehicles, which shape represents electric cars?

  A) A separate triangle and circle
  B) An overlapping area between the triangle and circle
  C) A triangle inside a circle
  D) A circle inside a triangle

Answer: B) An overlapping area between the triangle and circle

Explanation: The overlapping area between the triangle and circle represents entities that are both cars (triangle) and electric vehicles (circle), which would be electric cars.

Question 7: Number Series

Prompt: What comes next in the sequence: 5, 10, 20, 40, ...?

   A) 60
   B) 80
   C) 100
   D) 120

Answer: B) 80

Explanation: This is a series where each number is multiplied by 2. So, 40 x 2 = 80.

Question 8: Number Series

Prompt: Identify the next number in the series: 1, 4, 9, 16, ...?

   A) 20
   B) 25
   C) 30
   D) 36

Answer: B) 25

Explanation: This series represents the squares of natural numbers. Following this pattern, the next number is 5^2, which is 25.

Question 9: Geometric Comparisons

Prompt: If a square has a side of length 4, what is its area?

A) 8
B) 12
C) 16
D) 20

Answer: C) 16

Explanation: The area of a square is calculated as side length squared. So, for a side of length 4, the area is $4^2 = 16$.

Question 10: Non-Verbal Reasoning

Prompt: In a sequence of shapes, a circle is followed by a square, which is followed by a triangle, repeating in this order. If the sequence starts with a circle, what is the fifth shape?

A) Circle
B) Square
C) Triangle
D) Cannot be determined

Answer: B) Square

Explanation: Following the sequence (circle, square, triangle), the fifth shape will be a square (1st - circle, 2nd - square, 3rd - triangle, 4th - circle, 5th - square).

Question 11: Number Series

Prompt: Complete the series: 2, 6, 12, 20, __?

A) 28
B) 30
C) 32
D) 35

Answer: B) 30

Explanation: The pattern is adding consecutive even numbers (2, 4, 6, 8, ...). Thus, 20 + 10 (the next even number) = 30.

Question 12: Geometric Comparisons

Prompt: A rectangle has a length of 8 and a width of 3. What is its perimeter?

A) 22
B) 24
C) 26
D) 28

Answer: A) 22

Explanation: The perimeter of a rectangle is calculated as 2(length + width). So, 2(8 + 3) = 22.

Question 13: Non-Verbal Reasoning

Prompt: If a blue circle represents dogs and a red square represents pets, which color and shape would represent dogs that are not pets?

A) Blue square
B) Red circle
C) Blue circle only
D) Blue circle overlapping with red square

Answer: C) Blue circle only

Explanation: Dogs that are not pets would be represented only by the blue circle (dogs), without overlapping with the red square (pets).

Question 14: Number Series

Prompt: What is the next number in this sequence: 3, 9, 27, 81, ...?

   A) 162
   B) 243
   C) 324
   D) 405

Answer: B) 243

Explanation: This sequence follows the pattern of multiplying each number by 3 (3, 3x3, 9x3, 27x3, ...). Thus, the next number is 81 x 3 = 243.

Question 15: Number Series

Prompt: Find the next number in the series: 5, 11, 17, 23, ...?

   A) 27
   B) 29

C) 31
D) 35

Answer: B) 29

Explanation: This series increases by 6 each time (5 + 6 = 11, 11 + 6 = 17, etc.). Therefore, the next number is 23 + 6 = 29.

Question 16: Geometric Comparisons

Prompt: How many edges does a cube have?

A) 6
B) 8
C) 12
D) 16

Answer: C) 12

Explanation: A cube has 12 edges. It has 6 faces, but each face is a square with 4 edges, and each edge is shared between two faces.

Question 17: Non-Verbal Reasoning

Prompt: If square represents animals and triangle represents mammals, which shape would represent non-mammal animals?

A) Square overlapping with triangle
B) Triangle outside square
C) Square not overlapping with triangle
D) Circle

Answer: C) Square not overlapping with triangle

Explanation: Non-mammal animals would be represented by the part of the square (animals) that does not overlap with the triangle (mammals).

Question 18: Number Series

Prompt: What comes next in the sequence: 2, 6, 18, 54, ...?

A) 108
B) 162
C) 164
D) 216

Answer: B) 162

Explanation: Each number in the series is multiplied by 3 to get the next number (2 x 3 = 6, 6 x 3 = 18, 18 x 3 = 54). Thus, 54 x 3 = 162.

Question 19: Geometric Comparisons

Prompt: The perimeter of a rectangle is 30 cm. If the length is 10 cm, what is the width?

A) 5 cm
B) 7.5 cm
C) 10 cm
D) 15 cm

Answer: A) 5 cm

Explanation: Perimeter of a rectangle is 2(length + width). Given 30 = 2(10 + width), solving for width gives width = 5 cm.

Question 20: Non-Verbal Reasoning

Prompt: If 'circle' represents 'trees' and 'rectangle' represents 'evergreens,' which shape represents 'evergreen trees'?

A) Circle only

B) Rectangle only

C) Overlapping area between circle and rectangle

D) Separate circle and rectangle

Answer: C) Overlapping area between circle and rectangle

Explanation: Evergreen trees would be represented by the overlap between 'trees' (circle) and 'evergreens' (rectangle).

Question 21: Number Series

Prompt: Complete the series: 1, 1, 2, 3, 5, 8, __?

A) 11

B) 12

C) 13

D) 15

Answer: C) 13

Explanation: This is the Fibonacci series, where each number is the sum of the two preceding ones (1+1=2, 1+2=3, 2+3=5, 3+5=8). Thus, 8+5 = 13.

Question 22: Number Series

Prompt: What is the next number in the series: 3, 6, 12, 24, ...?

A) 36
B) 48
C) 50
D) 52

Answer: B) 48

Explanation: Each number in the series is doubled to get the next number. Therefore, the next number after 24 is 24 x 2 = 48.

Question 23: Geometric Comparisons

Prompt: If a triangle has a base of 6 cm and a height of 4 cm, what is its area?

A) 10 cm²
B) 12 cm²
C) 24 cm²
D) 48 cm²

Answer: B) 12 cm²

Explanation: The area of a triangle is given by $1/2 \times$ base $\times$ height. So, the area is $1/2 \times 6 \times 4 = 12$ cm².

Question 24: Non-Verbal Reasoning

Prompt: If a circle symbolizes planets and a cross symbolizes planets with moons, what does a circle with a cross represent?

  A) All planets
  B) Planets without moons
  C) Planets with moons
  D) Moons only

Answer: C) Planets with moons

Explanation: A circle with a cross combines the symbols for planets and planets with moons, thus representing planets with moons.

Question 25: Number Series

Prompt: Complete the sequence: 4, 9, 16, 25, __?

  A) 30
  B) 34
  C) 36

D) 49

Answer: C) 36

Explanation: This sequence follows the pattern of square numbers ($2^2 = 4$, $3^2 = 9$, $4^2 = 16$, $5^2 = 25$). The next square number is 6^2, which is 36.

Question 26: Geometric Comparisons

Prompt: What is the sum of the angles in a triangle?

A) 90 degrees
B) 180 degrees
C) 270 degrees
D) 360 degrees

Answer: B) 180 degrees

Explanation: The sum of the angles in any triangle is always 180 degrees.

Question 27: Non-Verbal Reasoning

Prompt: If blue circles represent oceans and green triangles represent forests, what does a green circle represent?

A) Oceans only
B) Forests only
C) Forested Oceans
D) Neither oceans nor forests

Answer: D) Neither oceans nor forests

Explanation: A green circle combines the color for forests (green) with the shape for oceans (circle), but it does not match the symbol for either category exactly. Thus, it represents neither.

Question 28: Number Series

Prompt: What comes next in the sequence: 1, 4, 9, 16, 25, 36, ...?

A) 45
B) 48
C) 49
D) 56

Answer: C) 49

Explanation: This sequence consists of consecutive square numbers (1^2, 2^2, 3^2, 4^2, 5^2, 6^2). The next number is the square of 7, which is 49 (7^2).

Question 29: Number Series

Prompt: What is the next number in the series: 10, 20, 40, 80, ...?

    A) 100
    B) 120
    C) 160
    D) 200

Answer: C) 160

Explanation: This series doubles each number to get the next. So, 80 doubled is 160.

Question 30: Basic Arithmetic

Prompt: If you buy 3 pencils for $0.50 each, how much do you spend in total?

    A) $0.50
    B) $1.00
    C) $1.50
    D) $2.00

Answer: C) $1.50

Explanation: Each pencil costs $0.50, so 3 pencils cost 3 x $0.50 = $1.50.

Question 31: Geometry

Prompt: A rectangle has a length of 5 cm and a width of 3 cm. What is its area?

   A) 8 cm²
   B) 15 cm²
   C) 16 cm²
   D) 20 cm²

Answer: B) 15 cm²

Explanation: Area of a rectangle is length x width. So, 5 cm x 3 cm = 15 cm².

Question 32: Non-Verbal Reasoning

Prompt: If a blue square represents cats and a red circle represents pets, which symbol would represent cats that are not pets?

   A) Blue square only
   B) Red circle only

C) Overlapping area between blue square and red circle

D) Blue square overlapping with red circle

Answer: A) Blue square only

Explanation: Cats that are not pets would be represented by the blue square (cats) alone, without overlapping with the red circle (pets).

Question 33: Number Series

Prompt: What comes next in the sequence: 2, 4, 8, 16, 32, ...?

A) 48
B) 54
C) 64
D) 72

Answer: C) 64

Explanation: Each number in the sequence is doubled to get the next. Hence, the next number after 32 is 32 x 2 = 64.

Question 34: Basic Arithmetic

Prompt: Divide 150 by 5.

A) 25
B) 30
C) 35
D) 40

Answer: B) 30

Explanation: 150 divided by 5 is 30.

Question 35: Geometry

Prompt: If the side of a square is 4 cm, what is its perimeter?

A) 8 cm
B) 12 cm
C) 16 cm
D) 20 cm

Answer: C) 16 cm

Explanation: Perimeter of a square is 4 times the length of one side. So, 4 x 4 cm = 16 cm.

Question 36: Number Series

Prompt: What is the next number in the series: 1, 3, 6, 10, ...?

A) 13
B) 15
C) 18
D) 21

Answer: B) 15

Explanation: This is a series where each number increases by an incrementally larger amount (1, 2, 3, 4, ...). The pattern is: 1, 1+2=3, 3+3=6, 6+4=10, and the next is 10+5=15.

Question 37: Basic Arithmetic

Prompt: If you have 24 apples and you divide them equally among 4 friends, how many apples does each friend get?

A) 4
B) 5
C) 6
D) 8

Answer: C) 6

Explanation: Dividing 24 apples equally among 4 friends means each friend gets 24 / 4 = 6 apples.

Question 38: Geometry

Prompt: A triangle has sides of lengths 3 cm, 4 cm, and 5 cm. Is it a right triangle?

A) Yes
B) No
C) Cannot be determined
D) Irrelevant

Answer: A) Yes

Explanation: According to the Pythagorean theorem, if the square of the longest side equals the sum of the squares of the other two sides, the triangle is right-angled. Here, $5^2 = 3^2 + 4^2$, so it's a right triangle.

Question 39: Non-Verbal Reasoning

Prompt: If a circle represents cars and a square represents red objects, what does a red car represent?

A) Circle only
B) Square only
C) Overlapping area between circle and square
D) Non-overlapping area between circle and square

Answer: C) Overlapping area between circle and square

Explanation: A red car would be represented by the area where the circle (cars) and the square (red objects) overlap.

Question 40: Number Series

Prompt: Complete the sequence: 5, 10, 20, 40, __?

A) 60
B) 70
C) 80
D) 90

Answer: C) 80

Explanation: The sequence doubles each number to get the next. Thus, the next number after 40 is 40 x 2 = 80.

Question 41: Basic Arithmetic

Prompt: If a shirt costs $20 and you have a 25% discount coupon, how much will you pay?

A) $5
B) $10
C) $15
D) $25

Answer: C) $15

Explanation: A 25% discount on a $20 shirt means you save 25/100 x 20 = $5. So, the price you pay is $20 - $5 = $15.

Question 42: Geometry

Prompt: What is the sum of the interior angles of a quadrilateral?

A) 180 degrees
B) 270 degrees

C) 360 degrees
D) 540 degrees

Answer: C) 360 degrees

Explanation: The sum of the interior angles of a quadrilateral (a four-sided polygon) is always 360 degrees.

Question 43: Number Series

Prompt: What is the next number in the series: 2, 4, 8, 16, 32, ...?

A) 48
B) 64
C) 96
D) 128

Answer: B) 64

Explanation: This is a geometric series where each number is multiplied by 2 to obtain the next number. Hence, 32 multiplied by 2 equals 64.

Question 44: Geometry

Prompt: If the perimeter of a square is 24 cm, what is the length of one side?

A) 4 cm
B) 6 cm
C) 8 cm
D) 12 cm

Answer: B) 6 cm

Explanation: The perimeter of a square is 4 times the length of one side. So, 24 cm divided by 4 equals 6 cm for each side.

Question 45: Arithmetic Reasoning

Prompt: A baker used 3/4 of a bag of flour. If the bag had 8 pounds of flour, how much flour did the baker use?

A) 2 pounds
B) 4 pounds
C) 6 pounds
D) 8 pounds

Answer: C) 6 pounds

Explanation: 3/4 of 8 pounds equals (3/4) * 8 = 6 pounds of flour.

Question 46: Number Series

Prompt: Identify the next number in the series: 3, 9, 27, 81, ...?

A) 162
B) 243
C) 324
D) 405

Answer: B) 243

Explanation: Each number in this series is multiplied by 3 to obtain the next number. So, 81 multiplied by 3 equals 243.

Question 47: Geometry

Prompt: A triangle has sides of 5 cm, 12 cm, and 13 cm. Is this a right triangle?

A) Yes
B) No
C) Cannot be determined

Answer: A) Yes

Explanation: According to the Pythagorean theorem, if the square of the longest side (13 cm) equals the sum of the squares of the other two sides, then it's a right triangle. Here, $13^2 = 5^2 + 12^2$, so it's a right triangle.

Question 48: Arithmetic Reasoning

Prompt: If a car travels at a speed of 60 miles per hour, how far will it travel in 15 minutes?

  A) 15 miles
  B) 30 miles
  C) 45 miles
  D) 60 miles

Answer: A) 15 miles

Explanation: At 60 miles per hour, in one hour the car travels 60 miles. Therefore, in 15 minutes (1/4 of an hour), it will travel 60 * 1/4 = 15 miles.

Question 49: Number Series

Prompt: Complete the sequence: 1, 1, 2, 3, 5, 8, __?

A) 11
B) 12
C) 13
D) 15

Answer: C) 13

Explanation: This sequence is the Fibonacci series, where each number is the sum of the two preceding ones. Hence, the next number is 8 + 5 = 13.

Question 50: Arithmetic Reasoning

Prompt: If you divide 36 by half and add 10, what is the result?

A) 28
B) 46
C) 64
D) 82

Answer: D) 82

Explanation: Dividing by half is equivalent to multiplying by 2 (as dividing by a fraction is the same as multiplying by its reciprocal). So, 36 divided by 1/2 is 36 * 2 = 72. Adding 10 gives 72 + 10 = 82.

Question 51: Geometry

Prompt: The radius of a circle is 4 cm. What is the area of the circle? (Use π = 3.14)

  A) 16 cm²
  B) 25.12 cm²
  C) 50.24 cm²
  D) 100.48 cm²

Answer: C) 50.24 cm²

Explanation: The area of a circle is πr^2, where r is the radius. So, the area is $3.14 * 4^2 = 3.14 * 16 = 50.24$ cm².

Question 52: Number Series

Prompt: What comes next in the sequence: 1, 2, 4, 7, 11, ...?

  A) 15
  B) 16
  C) 17
  D) 18

Answer: B) 16

Explanation: The pattern in this series is each number is the sum of the previous number and an incrementally increasing number: 1, 1+1=2, 2+2=4, 4+3=7, 7+4=11, and 11+5=16. Thus, the next number is 16.

SECTION 3: Reading Comprehension

For the Reading Comprehension section of the HSPT, it's important to practice with a variety of passages and question types to improve reading speed, comprehension, and interpretation skills.

Engaging with diverse reading materials and questioning styles will prepare you effectively for the Reading Comprehension challenges of the HSPT.

Question 1

Passage: "The forest was alive with the sounds of nature. Birds chirped in the canopy above, and a gentle breeze rustled through the leaves. Julie paused, taking in the beauty around her. She always felt at peace in the forest, away from the hustle and bustle of city life. Here, she could think and breathe.

She sat down on a fallen log, closed her eyes, and listened to the natural symphony."

Question: What is the main purpose of this passage?

  A) To describe the dangers of forest life
  B) To illustrate Julie's love for nature
  C) To provide a detailed guide to bird sounds
  D) To compare city life with life in the forest

Answer: B) To illustrate Julie's love for nature

Explanation: The passage focuses on Julie's experience in the forest, highlighting how she finds peace and enjoyment in the natural setting. There is no comparison between city and forest life, nor is there a detailed guide to bird sounds or any mention of dangers in the forest.

Question 2

Passage: "In a small village nestled in the mountains, there was a tradition that every spring, the villagers would gather to plant new trees around their homes. This practice had been a part of their culture for generations, believed to bring good fortune and protect the village from natural disasters. Each family took pride in nurturing these trees, ensuring they grew strong and healthy. Over time, this tradition not only beautified the village but also helped create a strong sense of community among the villagers."

Question: What can be inferred about the village's tree-planting tradition?

   A) It was a recent initiative to improve the environment.
   B) It was a long-standing cultural practice with multiple benefits.
   C) The villagers were required to plant trees by law.
   D) The practice was intended to increase tourism in the village.

Answer: B) It was a long-standing cultural practice with multiple benefits.

Explanation: The passage states that the tree-planting tradition had been part of the village culture for generations and mentions its benefits, such as bringing good fortune, protecting from disasters, enhancing beauty, and fostering community spirit. There is no indication that it was a recent initiative, legally mandated, or intended for tourism.

Question 3:

Passage Concept: A discussion about the migration patterns of monarch butterflies and the environmental factors that influence their journey.

Question: According to the passage, what is a significant factor in the migration of monarch butterflies?

  A) Changes in global trade patterns
  B) Urbanization and its effects on wildlife
  C) Seasonal changes in weather and temperature
  D) The introduction of new butterfly species

Answer: C) Seasonal changes in weather and temperature

Explanation: The passage focuses on the migration of monarch butterflies, indicating that environmental factors like weather and temperature are crucial in their migration process.

Question 4:

Passage Concept: An article about the history of the telescope and its impact on astronomy, highlighting key developments over the centuries.

Question: What is the main theme of the passage?

  A) The technical specifications of different telescopes
  B) The challenges faced in the early stages of telescope development
  C) The evolution of the telescope and its impact on astronomy
  D) The biographies of famous astronomers

Answer: C) The evolution of the telescope and its impact on astronomy

Explanation: Given the focus on the historical development of the telescope and its influence on the field of astronomy, the passage mainly explores the evolution of this instrument and its significance.

Question 5:

Passage Concept: A personal narrative about growing up in a multilingual family and the advantages and challenges of learning multiple languages from a young age.

Question: What aspect of multilingual upbringing is emphasized in the passage?

A) The cognitive difficulties in learning multiple languages

B) The cultural benefits and challenges of a multilingual environment

C) The rarity of multilingual families in modern society

D) The economic advantages of knowing multiple languages

Answer: B) The cultural benefits and challenges of a multilingual environment

Explanation: The passage's focus on a personal experience of growing up in a multilingual family suggests an emphasis on the cultural aspects, including both the benefits and challenges encountered in such an environment.

Question 6:

Passage Concept: A description of a community project to restore a local park, emphasizing the collaborative efforts of residents and the positive changes in the neighborhood.

Question: What is the passage primarily highlighting?

A) The decline of public spaces in urban areas
B) The challenges of managing community projects
C) The success of a community in improving a local park
D) The need for more government funding in public projects

Answer: C) The success of a community in improving a local park

Explanation: The passage focuses on a successful community effort to restore a local park, emphasizing the positive impact of collaborative work on neighborhood improvement.

Question 7:

Passage Concept: An informative article about the importance of bees in the ecosystem, discussing their role in pollination and the threats they face.

Question: According to the passage, why are bees considered crucial for the ecosystem?

A) Their ability to produce honey
B) Their role in the pollination of plants
C) Their large population numbers
D) Their contribution to biodiversity

Answer: B) Their role in the pollination of plants

Explanation: The passage discusses bees' importance in the ecosystem, particularly emphasizing their critical role in pollinating plants, which is vital for the health of many ecosystems.

Question 8:

Passage Concept: A historical account of the construction of the Transcontinental Railroad and its impact on American expansion and commerce.

Question: What aspect of the Transcontinental Railroad does the passage mainly discuss?

  A) The engineering challenges during its construction
  B) Its impact on American expansion and commerce
  C) The lifestyles of workers who built the railroad
  D) The technological innovations of train travel

Answer: B) Its impact on American expansion and commerce

Explanation: The passage focuses on the broader implications of the Transcontinental Railroad, particularly its significant impact on the expansion and commercial development of the United States.

Question 9:

Passage Concept: An article discussing the phenomenon of urban farming and its role in promoting sustainable living in cities.

Question: What is the primary focus of the passage?

  A) The challenges of living in urban areas
  B) The benefits of urban farming for sustainable living
  C) A comparison between rural and urban farming techniques
  D) The economic impact of farming in cities

Answer: B) The benefits of urban farming for sustainable living

Explanation: The passage concentrates on urban farming and its contribution to sustainability in urban environments, highlighting how it helps promote a more sustainable lifestyle in cities.

Question 10:

Passage Concept: A narrative about an individual's first experience stargazing and the sense of wonder it instilled, leading to a lifelong interest in astronomy.

Question: According to the passage, what impact did stargazing have on the individual?

  A) It was a one-time event with no lasting interest
  B) It created a deep sense of confusion about the universe
  C) It sparked a lifelong passion for astronomy
  D) It led to a career in space engineering

Answer: C) It sparked a lifelong passion for astronomy

Explanation: The passage describes how the individual's first experience of stargazing evoked a sense of wonder and sparked a lasting interest in astronomy, leading to a lifelong passion for the subject.

Question 11:

Passage Concept: A description of the process of photosynthesis in plants and its importance for both plants and the environment.

Question: What is the primary topic of the passage?

  A) The various types of plants in an ecosystem
  B) The environmental benefits of planting trees
  C) The process of photosynthesis and its importance
  D) The relationship between sunlight and plant growth

Answer: C) The process of photosynthesis and its importance

Explanation: The passage focuses on explaining the process of photosynthesis in plants and underscores its significance for plants themselves and the broader environment.

Question 12:

Passage Concept: An essay about the impact of technology on communication, emphasizing both the advantages and challenges it brings to interpersonal relationships.

Question: What is the essay primarily concerned with?

  A) The history of technological advancements
  B) The effects of technology on personal communication
  C) The economic impact of technology on society
  D) The technical aspects of communication devices

Answer: B) The effects of technology on personal communication

Explanation: The essay focuses on how technology influences the way people communicate, discussing both the positive and negative aspects of this impact on interpersonal relationships.

Question13:

Passage Concept: A discussion about the conservation efforts to protect endangered species, highlighting various strategies used to preserve biodiversity.

Question: According to the passage, what is a primary goal of conservation efforts?

  A) To promote eco-tourism
  B) To protect endangered species

C) To regulate urban development

D) To increase agricultural productivity

Answer: B) To protect endangered species

Explanation: The passage discusses conservation strategies, particularly emphasizing the importance of protecting species that are at risk of extinction, thereby focusing on preserving biodiversity.

Question 14:

Passage Concept: A biographical piece about a renowned scientist's journey, including their early interest in science, challenges faced, and major achievements.

Question: What aspect of the scientist's life is mainly highlighted in the piece?

   A) Their personal hobbies and interests outside of science

   B) Their educational background and academic degrees

   C) The journey and accomplishments in their scientific career

   D) Their role as a teacher and mentor to students

Answer: C) The journey and accomplishments in their scientific career

Explanation: The biographical piece centers on the scientist's career path, from initial interest in science through the challenges encountered and ultimately their significant contributions and achievements in the field.

Question 15:

Passage Concept: An article about the resurgence of traditional crafts in modern times, exploring how these skills are being revived and appreciated in a digital age.

Question: What is the main theme of the article?

   A) The decline of traditional crafts in the face of technology
   B) The challenges in learning ancient crafting techniques
   C) The revival and growing appreciation of traditional crafts
   D) The economic impact of crafts on modern markets

Answer: C) The revival and growing appreciation of traditional crafts

Explanation: The article discusses the renewed interest and value found in traditional crafts, highlighting how they are being embraced and respected even in a digital era.

Question 16:

Passage Concept: A story about a young athlete's determination to excel in a sport despite facing numerous obstacles, focusing on their journey and ultimate success.

Question: What is the central focus of the story?

    A) The technical aspects of the sport
    B) The athlete's personal life and family
    C) The athlete's perseverance and eventual success
    D) The competitive nature of sports

Answer: C) The athlete's perseverance and eventual success

Explanation: The story emphasizes the athlete's relentless determination and the challenges they overcome, culminating in their eventual success in the sport.

Question 17:

Passage Concept: A descriptive piece about the Amazon rainforest, detailing the diverse flora and fauna, and the ecosystem's crucial role in the global environment.

Question: What aspect of the Amazon rainforest does the passage primarily describe?

  A) The threats posed by deforestation and climate change
  B) The commercial potential of the rainforest's resources
  C) The diversity of life and the importance of the ecosystem
  D) The experience of travelers and explorers in the rainforest

Answer: C) The diversity of life and the importance of the ecosystem

Explanation: The passage mainly focuses on the rich biodiversity present in the Amazon rainforest and underscores its significance in maintaining global ecological balance.

Question 18:

Passage Concept: An exploration of the impact of social media on modern communication, focusing on how it has changed the way people interact and share information.

Question: What is the primary focus of the passage?

  A) The technical development of social media platforms
  B) The historical evolution of communication
  C) The influence of social media on communication practices
  D) Privacy concerns associated with online interactions

Answer: C) The influence of social media on communication practices

Explanation: The passage primarily discusses the significant impact that social media has had on modern communication methods, altering the way people interact and disseminate information.

Question 19:

Passage Concept: A narrative about a family's annual camping trip, detailing their experiences and the lasting memories they create together in nature.

Question: What is the main theme of the narrative?

  A) The challenges of outdoor survival skills
  B) The environmental impact of camping
  C) The value of family bonding during outdoor activities
  D) The comparison of different camping styles

Answer: C) The value of family bonding during outdoor activities

Explanation: The narrative centers on the experiences of a family on their camping trip, highlighting the importance and impact of such activities in fostering family bonds and creating cherished memories.

Question 20:

Passage Concept: A discussion about renewable energy sources, specifically focusing on solar and wind power, and their role in addressing environmental challenges.

Question: According to the passage, what is a significant benefit of solar and wind energy?

   A) They are more cost-effective than traditional energy sources
   B) They offer a solution to reduce environmental impact
   C) They are easier to implement than other renewable resources
   D) They have a longer history of use than other energy forms

Answer: B) They offer a solution to reduce environmental impact

Explanation: The passage highlights solar and wind power as key renewable energy sources, emphasizing their role in helping to mitigate environmental challenges such as pollution and climate change.

Question 21:

Passage Concept: An article about the resurgence of community gardens in urban areas, focusing on how they promote social interaction and local food production.

Question: What is the main point of the article?

   A) The economic benefits of urban agriculture
   B) The challenges in maintaining community gardens
   C) The rise of community gardens and their social and environmental benefits
   D) The history of gardening practices in urban settings

Answer: C) The rise of community gardens and their social and environmental benefits

Explanation: The article emphasizes the increasing popularity of community gardens in cities and their role in enhancing social bonds and encouraging local food production, highlighting their social and environmental advantages.

Question 22:

Passage Concept: A story about a young musician overcoming stage fright to deliver a stunning performance, emphasizing personal growth and confidence.

Question: What is the central theme of the story?

A) The competitive nature of musical performances
B) Overcoming personal challenges to achieve success
C) The technical aspects of musical composition
D) The importance of formal musical education

Answer: B) Overcoming personal challenges to achieve success

Explanation: The story focuses on the young musician's journey to overcome stage fright, illustrating how facing and conquering personal fears leads to a triumphant and confidence-boosting performance.

Question 23:

Passage Concept: An informative piece about the evolution of space exploration, from early telescopes to modern space missions.

Question: According to the passage, what has been a significant development in the field of space exploration?

A) The privatization of space travel
B) The transition from earth-based to space-based telescopes

C) The discovery of life on other planets

D) The evolution from early astronomical tools to advanced space missions

Answer: D) The evolution from early astronomical tools to advanced space missions

Explanation: The passage outlines the progress in space exploration, highlighting the journey from the initial use of basic telescopes to the complexity of contemporary space missions.

Question 24:

Passage Concept: A reflective essay about the importance of teamwork in sports, highlighting how collaboration and mutual support lead to success.

Question: What is the main focus of the essay?

A) The physical demands and skills required in sports

B) The role of individual talent in sports success

C) The significance of teamwork in achieving sports goals

D) The comparison between individual and team sports

Answer: C) The significance of teamwork in achieving sports goals

Explanation: The essay emphasizes the crucial role of teamwork in sports, discussing how cooperation and support among team members are key to attaining success in sporting endeavors.

Question 25:

Passage Concept: An article about the ancient art of pottery, exploring its historical significance and the techniques used in different cultures.

Question: According to the passage, what aspect of pottery is primarily discussed?

   A) The economic impact of pottery in the modern world
   B) The historical and cultural significance of pottery-making
   C) The technological advancements in pottery production
   D) The use of pottery in contemporary art

Answer: B) The historical and cultural significance of pottery-making

Explanation: The article delves into the history of pottery, highlighting its importance and the diverse techniques employed in various cultures, thus focusing on its cultural and historical aspects.

Question 26:

Passage Concept: A piece describing the process of photosynthesis in plants and its critical role in the Earth's ecosystem.

Question: What is the primary topic of the passage?

A) The environmental challenges faced by plant species
B) The technical details of botanical studies
C) The process of photosynthesis and its ecological importance
D) The relationship between plants and animals

Answer: C) The process of photosynthesis and its ecological importance

Explanation: The passage focuses on explaining how photosynthesis works in plants and its significance in maintaining ecological balance, emphasizing its vital role in the Earth's ecosystem.

Question 27:

Passage Concept: An account of the first moon landing, describing the astronauts' experiences and the significance of this event in space exploration history.

Question: What is the primary focus of the passage?

  A) The technical details of spacecraft engineering
  B) The personal backgrounds of the astronauts involved
  C) The historical significance and experiences of the moon landing
  D) The future potential for interstellar travel

Answer: C) The historical significance and experiences of the moon landing

Explanation: The passage is centered on the momentous event of the first moon landing, highlighting the experiences of the astronauts and the milestone's importance in the history of space exploration.

Question 28:

Passage Concept: A discussion about the growing popularity of electric vehicles (EVs), focusing on their environmental benefits and the challenges they face.

Question: According to the passage, what is a significant benefit of electric vehicles?

   A) They are more cost-effective in the long term
   B) They offer an environmentally friendly alternative to traditional cars
   C) They provide a smoother driving experience
   D) They require less maintenance than conventional vehicles

Answer: B) They offer an environmentally friendly alternative to traditional cars

Explanation: The passage discusses the increasing adoption of EVs, particularly emphasizing their role as a more environmentally friendly option compared to traditional gasoline-powered vehicles.

Question 29:

Passage Concept: A feature about the revival of traditional folk music, exploring how it connects people to their cultural heritage and fosters community.

Question: What aspect of traditional folk music is primarily highlighted in the feature?

  A) Its complexity and varied instrumentation
  B) Its role in connecting people to their cultural roots
  C) The commercial success of folk music artists
  D) The influence of modern genres on folk music

Answer: B) Its role in connecting people to their cultural roots

Explanation: The feature sheds light on how traditional folk music is experiencing a resurgence, serving as a means for individuals to connect with their cultural heritage and strengthen community ties.

Question 30:

Passage Concept: A detailed overview of the process of coffee production, from bean cultivation to brewing.

Question: What is the main topic of the passage?

   A) The economic impact of coffee trade
   B) The cultural significance of coffee drinking
   C) The environmental aspects of coffee farming
   D) The stages involved in coffee production

Answer: D) The stages involved in coffee production

Explanation: The passage gives a comprehensive look at how coffee is produced, describing each step from the initial cultivation of beans to the final process of brewing coffee.

Question 31:

Passage Concept: A story about an artist who uses recycled materials to create sculptures, focusing on the theme of sustainability in art.

Question: According to the story, what drives the artist's choice of materials?

A) The availability and cost-effectiveness of recycled materials
B) A desire to promote environmental sustainability through art
C) The challenge of working with unconventional materials
D) The influence of contemporary art trends

Answer: B) A desire to promote environmental sustainability through art

Explanation: The artist chooses recycled materials as a means of incorporating the theme of sustainability into their art, using their work to highlight environmental issues.

Question 32:

Passage Concept: An article discussing the impact of smartphones on modern-day personal communication, examining both the advantages and drawbacks.

Question: What is the primary concern addressed in the article?

A) The technological advancements in smartphone design

B) The influence of smartphones on face-to-face interactions

C) The cost of maintaining up-to-date smartphone technology

D) The role of smartphones in professional settings

Answer: B) The influence of smartphones on face-to-face interactions

Explanation: The article centers on how smartphones have affected the way individuals communicate in their personal lives, specifically discussing the changes in direct, in-person interactions.

Question 33:

Passage Concept: An exploration of the importance of coral reefs to marine ecosystems, detailing their role in supporting a diverse range of marine life.

Question: What is the passage primarily about?

A) The recreational benefits of coral reefs for scuba diving

B) The role of coral reefs in supporting marine biodiversity

C) The process of coral formation and growth

D) The impact of climate change on ocean currents

Answer: B) The role of coral reefs in supporting marine biodiversity

Explanation: The passage focuses on the critical importance of coral reefs in marine ecosystems, especially their role in providing habitat and support for a wide variety of marine species.

Question 34:

Passage Concept: A historical account of the invention of the printing press and its profound impact on literacy and the spread of information.

Question: According to the passage, what was a significant outcome of the printing press invention?

A) The increase in handmade book production
B) The standardization of language in printed materials
C) The widespread dissemination of information and rise in literacy
D) The decline of oral storytelling traditions

Answer: C) The widespread dissemination of information and rise in literacy

Explanation: The invention of the printing press led to a revolution in how information was disseminated, making books more accessible and significantly contributing to increased literacy rates.

Question 35:

Passage Concept: A description of a traditional festival in a small town, highlighting the customs, music, and food that define this annual event.

Question: What is the focus of the passage?

  A) The economic benefits of the festival to the town
  B) The specific foods served at the festival
  C) The cultural significance and traditions of the festival
  D) The historical origins of festivals in general

Answer: C) The cultural significance and traditions of the festival

Explanation: The passage describes the various aspects of the festival, particularly emphasizing its cultural importance to the town and the traditional customs, music, and food that characterize the event.

Question 36:

Passage Concept: An article on the global impact of renewable energy sources, focusing on how they are transforming energy consumption and reducing environmental degradation.

Question: What is the central theme of the article?

   A) The technical challenges in harnessing renewable energy
   B) The economic impact of shifting to renewable energy
   C) The global significance of adopting renewable energy sources
   D) The history of renewable energy development

Answer: C) The global significance of adopting renewable energy sources

Explanation: The article emphasizes the importance of renewable energy sources in changing global energy practices and their role in mitigating environmental issues, highlighting their worldwide impact.

Question 37:

Passage Concept: A memoir excerpt describing the author's childhood experiences in a coastal town, focusing on the lessons learned from life by the sea.

Question: What aspect of the author's childhood does the memoir primarily explore?

  A) The difficulties of growing up in a small town
  B) The influence of coastal life on the author's upbringing
  C) The author's academic journey in childhood
  D) The author's early interest in marine biology

Answer: B) The influence of coastal life on the author's upbringing

Explanation: The memoir reflects on the author's childhood in a coastal town, particularly focusing on how living by the sea shaped their early life experiences and lessons learned.

Question 38:

Passage Concept: A discussion about the rise of virtual reality technology and its applications in various fields such as education, medicine, and entertainment.

Question: According to the passage, what is a significant impact of virtual reality technology?

   A) Its role in replacing traditional education methods
   B) Its potential in diversifying experiences across different sectors
   C) Its contribution to the decline of conventional entertainment
   D) Its effect on interpersonal communication skills

Answer: B) Its potential in diversifying experiences across different sectors

Explanation: The passage outlines the expanding use of virtual reality technology, highlighting its ability to enhance and diversify experiences in education, medicine, entertainment, and other fields.

Question 39:

Passage Concept: An opinion piece on the importance of preserving historical landmarks, arguing for the need to maintain these sites for cultural and educational purposes.

Question: What is the main argument presented in the opinion piece?

A) Historical landmarks should be modernized

B) Preservation of historical landmarks is crucial for cultural heritage

C) Tourist attractions offer economic benefits

D) New construction should replace old landmarks for progress

Answer: B) Preservation of historical landmarks is crucial for cultural heritage

Explanation: The piece emphasizes the significance of maintaining historical landmarks, highlighting their value in terms of cultural heritage and education, rather than replacing them with modern structures.

Question 40:

Passage Concept: A feature article about urban green spaces, detailing their benefits for city dwellers and the environment, including mental health improvements and biodiversity support.

Question: According to the article, what are the primary benefits of urban green spaces?

A) Providing recreational facilities and sports areas

B) Enhancing mental health and supporting biodiversity

C) Increasing property values in urban areas

D) Serving as venues for social events

Answer: B) Enhancing mental health and supporting biodiversity

Explanation: The article focuses on the advantages of having green spaces in urban settings, particularly in terms of promoting mental well-being for residents and fostering ecological diversity.

Question 41:

Passage Concept: A travelog describing a journey through various countries in Southeast Asia, with insights into the diverse cultures, cuisines, and landscapes encountered.

Question: What is the primary focus of the travelog?

  A) The challenges of traveling in Southeast Asia

  B) A comparison of Southeast Asian countries with Western nations

  C) The unique cultural and culinary experiences in Southeast Asia

  D) Tips and advice for traveling on a budget

Answer: C) The unique cultural and culinary experiences in Southeast Asia

Explanation: The travelog captures the author's experiences in Southeast Asia, focusing on the rich cultural diversity, the various local cuisines, and the picturesque landscapes that characterize the region.

Question 42:

Passage Concept: An exploration of the significance of community libraries, focusing on their role as centers for learning, gathering, and cultural enrichment.

Question: What is the primary theme of the passage?

  A) The architectural evolution of library buildings
  B) The role of libraries as essential community hubs
  C) The financial challenges faced by public libraries
  D) The transition of libraries to digital platforms

Answer: B) The role of libraries as essential community hubs

Explanation: The passage highlights the importance of community libraries, not just as places for book lending but as vital centers for learning, social interaction, and cultural activities within communities.

Question 43:

Passage Concept: A personal essay about the writer's experience learning to cook traditional family recipes, reflecting on the connection between food and cultural heritage.

Question: According to the essay, what does learning to cook family recipes represent for the writer?

  A) A challenge to modernize traditional dishes
  B) An opportunity to connect with cultural roots
  C) A way to develop a potential culinary career
  D) A critique of contemporary cooking shows

Answer: B) An opportunity to connect with cultural roots

Explanation: The writer views learning traditional family recipes as a meaningful way to connect with their cultural heritage, allowing them to maintain and celebrate their family's culinary traditions.

Question 44:

Passage Concept: A report on the growing trend of urban farming, discussing how city dwellers are cultivating gardens in small spaces to grow their own food.

Question: What aspect of urban farming does the report primarily focus on?

  A) The techniques used in large-scale agricultural farming
  B) The challenges of finding space for farming in cities
  C) The benefits of city residents growing their own food
  D) The economic impact of reduced food transportation

Answer: C) The benefits of city residents growing their own food

Explanation: The report sheds light on the practice of urban farming, emphasizing the advantages for city dwellers who cultivate their own gardens, such as having fresh produce and the satisfaction of growing food in limited urban spaces.

Question 45:

Passage Concept: An analysis of the impact of digital technology on the music industry, including changes in how music is produced, distributed, and consumed.

Question: What is the main focus of the analysis?

   A) The historical development of musical instruments
   B) The influence of digital technology on the music industry
   C) The decline of live musical performances
   D) The financial aspects of the music production business

Answer: B) The influence of digital technology on the music industry

Explanation: The analysis centers on the transformative impact of digital technology in the music industry, addressing how production, distribution, and consumption of music have evolved in the digital era.

Question 46:

Passage Concept: A reflective piece about the importance of community sports programs in promoting teamwork and healthy lifestyles among youths.

Question: According to the piece, what is a significant benefit of community sports programs?

  A) They provide professional training for aspiring athletes
  B) They foster teamwork and healthy living among young people
  C) They are a primary source of entertainment for communities
  D) They help in scouting talent for national sports teams

Answer: B) They foster teamwork and healthy living among young people

Explanation: The piece emphasizes the role of community sports programs in encouraging teamwork and promoting healthy, active lifestyles among youths, highlighting these as key benefits.

Question 47:

Passage Concept: A discussion about the growing trend of using electric vehicles (EVs) in urban areas, focusing on environmental benefits and the challenges in infrastructure.

Question: What is the primary topic of the discussion?

  A) Comparing the performance of EVs to gasoline vehicles
  B) The environmental advantages and infrastructural challenges of EVs
  C) The cost-benefit analysis of owning an electric vehicle
  D) The future of transportation technology

Answer: B) The environmental advantages and infrastructural challenges of EVs

Explanation: The discussion revolves around the adoption of electric vehicles in cities, particularly highlighting their environmental benefits while also addressing the challenges related to charging infrastructure and support systems.

Question 48:

Passage Concept: A feature on the revival of traditional storytelling in modern culture, examining its role in preserving history and fostering a sense of community.

Question: What is the primary theme of the feature?

A) The techniques and formats of traditional storytelling
B) The resurgence of storytelling as a means of preserving cultural heritage
C) The decline of oral traditions in the face of digital media
D) The comparison of storytelling across different cultures

Answer: B) The resurgence of storytelling as a means of preserving cultural heritage

Explanation: The feature focuses on how traditional storytelling is experiencing a revival and is being used as a tool to preserve cultural history and enhance community bonds.

Question 49:

Passage Concept: An exploration of the challenges and rewards of mountain climbing, including personal anecdotes from experienced climbers.

Question: According to the passage, what is a significant aspect of mountain climbing?

A) The competitive nature of the sport
B) The physical and psychological challenges it presents
C) The technical aspects of climbing gear
D) The popularity of climbing as a recreational activity

Answer: B) The physical and psychological challenges it presents

Explanation: The passage delves into the complexities of mountain climbing, highlighting the physical endurance and mental fortitude required to overcome the challenges faced by climbers.

Question 50:

Passage Concept: A report on the effects of urbanization on local wildlife, discussing the adaptation of certain species to city environments.

Question: What is the main focus of the report?

A) The architectural development of urban areas
B) The adaptation of wildlife to urban settings
C) The impact of pollution on urban ecosystems
D) Strategies for wildlife conservation in cities

Answer: B) The adaptation of wildlife to urban settings

Explanation: The report centers on how certain wildlife species adjust to the conditions of urban environments, adapting their behaviors and survival strategies to thrive amidst urbanization.

Question 51:

Passage Concept: An article about the growing trend of community-based renewable energy projects, highlighting their role in promoting sustainable energy practices.

Question: What is the main focus of the article?

A) The technical challenges in implementing renewable energy
B) The role of community initiatives in promoting sustainable energy

C) The economic impact of renewable energy on local communities

D) Comparison between different types of renewable energy sources

Answer: B) The role of community initiatives in promoting sustainable energy

Explanation: The article discusses the importance of community-led renewable energy projects, emphasizing how they contribute to the adoption of sustainable energy practices at a local level.

Question 52:

Passage Concept: A narrative about a person's experience working in a wildlife sanctuary, focusing on the lessons learned about conservation and animal behavior.

Question: According to the narrative, what aspect of working at the sanctuary is emphasized?

A) The daily routines and tasks in animal care

B) Insights gained into wildlife conservation and animal behavior

C) The challenges of maintaining a wildlife sanctuary

D) The personal journey of becoming a wildlife expert

Answer: B) Insights gained into wildlife conservation and animal behavior

Explanation: The narrative highlights the individual's experiences at the wildlife sanctuary, particularly the valuable insights they gained regarding wildlife conservation and understanding animal behavior.

Question 53:

Passage Concept: An exploration of ancient navigation techniques used by sailors, discussing how they relied on stars, currents, and wind patterns.

Question: What is the primary topic of the exploration?

A) The history of maritime exploration
B) The evolution of modern navigation technology
C) Ancient techniques of navigation used by sailors
D) The role of astronomy in contemporary navigation

Answer: C) Ancient techniques of navigation used by sailors

Explanation: The passage focuses on the methods used by ancient sailors to navigate the seas, detailing how they utilized natural elements like stars, ocean currents, and wind patterns for guidance.

Question 54:

Passage Concept: A discussion about the rise of urban greenery and rooftop gardens in major cities, focusing on their environmental and social benefits.

Question: What is the central focus of the discussion?

   A) The architectural challenges of constructing rooftop gardens
   B) The environmental and community advantages of urban greenery
   C) The economic cost of maintaining urban gardens
   D) Comparison of different urban gardening techniques

Answer: B) The environmental and community advantages of urban greenery

Explanation: The passage explores the increasing prevalence of rooftop gardens and other forms of urban greenery, emphasizing their role in enhancing environmental quality and providing social benefits in urban areas.

Question 55:

Passage Concept: A historical account of the development of the internet and its transformation of global communication and information access.

Question: According to the passage, what has been a significant impact of the internet?

  A) The decline of traditional print media
  B) The transformation of global communication and information sharing
  C) The technical aspects of internet infrastructure
  D) The economic challenges posed by digital technologies

Answer: B) The transformation of global communication and information sharing

Explanation: The historical account focuses on how the advent of the internet revolutionized the way information is communicated and accessed worldwide, significantly altering global interaction and information dissemination.

Question 56:

Passage Concept: An article on the benefits of learning a second language, including cognitive advantages and the opportunity for cultural exchange.

Question: What is the main theme of the article?

  A) The difficulties associated with learning a new language
  B) The cognitive and cultural benefits of bilingualism
  C) The best methods for language teaching
  D) The career advantages of being multilingual

Answer: B) The cognitive and cultural benefits of bilingualism

Explanation: The article discusses the advantages of being bilingual, highlighting not only the cognitive benefits, such as improved memory and multitasking skills, but also the cultural enrichment that comes from understanding another language.

Question 57:

Passage Concept: An essay about the resurgence of vinyl records in the digital age, discussing their appeal in terms of sound quality and nostalgia.

Question: What is the main focus of the essay?

   A) The technical process of producing vinyl records
   B) The declining sales of digital music formats
   C) The reasons behind the renewed popularity of vinyl records
   D) The history of music recording technology

Answer: C) The reasons behind the renewed popularity of vinyl records

Explanation: The essay explores why vinyl records have regained popularity, emphasizing aspects like their unique sound quality and the nostalgic value they hold for many music enthusiasts.

Question 58:

Passage Concept: A report on the impact of community theaters on local arts scenes, highlighting their role in promoting arts and culture at the grassroots level.

Question: According to the report, what significant role do community theaters play?

  A) Providing a platform for experimental theater productions
  B) Enhancing the local economy through arts-related tourism
  C) Fostering arts and culture within the community
  D) Offering professional training for aspiring actors

Answer: C) Fostering arts and culture within the community

Explanation: The report discusses how community theaters contribute significantly to local arts scenes by nurturing arts and culture at a community level, serving as accessible venues for local talent and art enthusiasts.

Question 59:

Passage Concept: An exploration of advancements in renewable energy technologies, focusing on how innovations are shaping the future of sustainable energy.

Question: What is the primary topic of the exploration?

A) The comparison of renewable and non-renewable energy sources

B) The economic impact of transitioning to renewable energy

C) Recent technological advancements in renewable energy

D) The environmental challenges in implementing renewable energy

Answer: C) Recent technological advancements in renewable energy

Explanation: The focus of the exploration is on recent developments in renewable energy technology, highlighting how these innovations are driving progress in the field of sustainable energy solutions.

Question 60:

Passage Concept: A feature on the growth of urban wildlife conservation efforts, highlighting how cities are adapting to support various animal species.

Question: What is the main focus of the feature?

A) The challenges animals face in urban environments

B) Urban planning and its impact on wildlife habitats

C) The increasing efforts in urban wildlife conservation

D) The debate over the coexistence of humans and animals in cities

Answer: C) The increasing efforts in urban wildlife conservation

Explanation: The feature discusses the growing trend of wildlife conservation within urban areas, focusing on how cities are evolving and implementing measures to support and protect various animal species in urban settings.

Question 61:

Passage Concept: An article about the tradition of storytelling in indigenous cultures, exploring its role in preserving history and imparting moral values.

Question: According to the article, what is a significant aspect of storytelling in indigenous cultures?

A) Its entertainment value in community gatherings

B) Its function as a method of preserving history and values

C) The linguistic diversity of storytelling techniques

D) The commercial potential of traditional stories

Answer: B) Its function as a method of preserving history and values

Explanation: The article emphasizes the importance of storytelling in indigenous cultures, particularly its role in maintaining historical records and teaching moral and cultural values through generations.

Question 62:

Passage Concept: A discussion on the importance of public parks in urban areas, considering their role in community health and social well-being.

Question: What is the primary topic of the discussion?

A) The design and landscaping of urban parks

B) The role of public parks in promoting community health and well-being

C) The financial costs of maintaining public parks

D) The history of public parks in urban development

Answer: B) The role of public parks in promoting community health and well-being

Explanation: The discussion focuses on the value of public parks in urban areas, highlighting their significance in enhancing community health, providing spaces for social interaction, and contributing to the overall well-being of city residents.

SECTION 3: MATHEMATICS

Question 1: Basic Arithmetic

Prompt: If a train travels 240 miles in 4 hours, what is its average speed in miles per hour?

A) 40 mph
B) 60 mph
C) 80 mph
D) 100 mph

Answer: B) 60 mph

Explanation: Average speed is calculated by dividing the total distance by the total time. So, the average speed of the train is 240 miles / 4 hours = 60 mph.

Question 2: Algebra

Prompt: Solve for x in the equation: 3x - 5 = 16

    A) 7
    B) 9
    C) 11
    D) 21

Answer: A) 7

Explanation: To solve for x, first add 5 to both sides of the equation: 3x = 21. Then, divide both sides by 3: x = 21 / 3, which gives x = 7.

Question 3: Geometry

Prompt: What is the area of a rectangle with a length of 8 cm and a width of 3 cm?

    A) 11 cm²
    B) 24 cm²
    C) 22 cm²
    D) 48 cm²

Answer: B) 24 cm²

Explanation: The area of a rectangle is found by multiplying the length by the width. So, the area is 8 cm × 3 cm = 24 cm².

Question 4: Basic Arithmetic

Prompt: What is the sum of 357 and 168?

A) 515
B) 525
C) 535

D) 545

Answer: B) 525

Explanation: Adding the two numbers: 357 + 168 = 525.

Question 5: Algebra

Prompt: If $5y - 3 = 12$, what is the value of y?

A) 3
B) 5
C) 4

D) 2

Answer: A) 3

Explanation: Solve for y: 5y - 3 = 12. Add 3 to both sides: 5y = 15. Divide by 5: y = 15 / 5, which gives y = 3.

Question 6: Geometry

Prompt: A triangle has sides of 5 cm, 12 cm, and 13 cm. What type of triangle is it?

A) Equilateral
B) Isosceles
C) Scalene

D) Right

Answer: D) Right

Explanation: The triangle is a right triangle since $5^2 + 12^2 = 13^2$ (25 + 144 = 169).

Question 7: Basic Arithmetic

Prompt: Subtract 134 from 560.

A) 426
B) 436
C) 446

D) 456

Answer: A) 426

Explanation: Subtracting the numbers: 560 - 134 = 426.

Question 8: Algebra

Prompt: Solve for x: 2x + 4 = 14

A) 3
B) 4
C) 5

D) 6

Answer: C) 5

Explanation: First, subtract 4 from both sides: 2x = 10. Then, divide both sides by 2: x = 10 / 2, giving x = 5.

Question 9: Geometry

Prompt: The perimeter of a square is 36 cm. What is the length of one side?

A) 6 cm
B) 9 cm
C) 12 cm

D) 18 cm

Answer: B) 9 cm

Explanation: The perimeter of a square is four times the length of one side. So, one side equals the perimeter divided by 4: 36 cm / 4 = 9 cm.

Question 10: Data Interpretation

Prompt: In a class of 40 students, 15 play basketball, 10 play football, and the rest do not play any sports. How many students do not play any sports?

A) 15
B) 20
C) 25

D) 30

Answer: A) 15

Explanation: Total students playing sports: 15 (basketball) + 10 (football) = 25. So, students not playing any sports = 40 - 25 = 15.

Question 11: Basic Arithmetic

Prompt: Multiply 27 by 3.

A) 54
B) 81
C) 90

D) 108

Answer: B) 81

Explanation: Multiplying the numbers: 27 × 3 = 81.

Question 12: Algebra

Prompt: If 3a + 2 = 11, what is the value of a?

A) 2
B) 3
C) 4

D) 5

Answer: B) 3

Explanation: First, subtract 2 from both sides: 3a = 9. Then, divide by 3: a = 9 / 3, which gives a = 3.

Question 13: Geometry

Prompt: A rectangular garden measures 20 m by 15 m. What is its area?

A) 200 m²
B) 250 m²
C) 300 m²

D) 350 m²

Answer: C) 300 m²

Explanation: Area of a rectangle = length × width. So, the area is 20 m × 15 m = 300 m².

Question 14: Arithmetic

Prompt: Find the product of 8 and 12.

Answer: 96

Explanation: Multiplying the two numbers: 8 × 12 = 96.

Question 15: Algebra

Prompt: If $x + 4 = 9$, what is the value of x?

Answer: 5

Explanation: Solve for x: Subtract 4 from both sides to get $x = 9 - 4$, which gives $x = 5$.

Question 16: Geometry

Prompt: A circle has a radius of 7 cm. What is its area? (Use $\pi \approx 3.14$)

Answer: Approximately 153.86 cm²

Explanation: Area of a circle = πr^2. So, the area is $3.14 \times 7^2 \approx 153.86$ cm².

Question 17: Arithmetic

Prompt: What is 150% of 80?

Answer: 120

Explanation: 150% of 80 is $1.5 \times 80 = 120$.

Question 18: Algebra

Prompt: Solve for y in $4y - 7 = 9$.

Answer: 4

Explanation: Add 7 to both sides to get $4y = 16$, then divide by 4 to find $y = 4$.

Question 19: Geometry

Prompt: What is the volume of a cube with sides of length 5 cm?

Answer: 125 cm³

Explanation: Volume of a cube = side³. So, the volume is $5^3 = 125$ cm³.

Question 20: Arithmetic

Prompt: Subtract 567 from 890.

Answer: 323

Explanation: Subtracting the numbers: 890 - 567 = 323.

Question 21: Algebra

Prompt: If $2x = 14$, what is x?

Answer: 7

Explanation: Divide both sides by 2 to solve for x: $x = 14 / 2$, which gives $x = 7$.

Question 22: Geometry

Prompt: The perimeter of a rectangle is 60 meters. If the length is 20 meters, what is the width?

Answer: 10 meters

Explanation: Perimeter = 2(length + width). So, $60 = 2(20 + \text{width})$. Solving for width gives $\text{width} = 10$ meters.

Question 23: Arithmetic

Prompt: What is the result of $345 \div 5$?

Answer: 69

Explanation: Dividing the numbers: $345 \div 5 = 69$.

Question 24: Arithmetic

Prompt: Calculate the sum of 123 and 456.

Answer: 579

Explanation: Adding the two numbers: 123 + 456 = 579.

Question 25: Algebra

Prompt: Solve for x in the equation: 5x + 10 = 35.

Answer: 5

Explanation: First, subtract 10 from both sides: 5x = 25. Then, divide by 5: x = 25 / 5, giving x = 5.

Question 26: Geometry

Prompt: What is the perimeter of a square with a side length of 9 cm?

Answer: 36 cm

Explanation: Perimeter of a square = 4 × side length. So, the perimeter is 4 × 9 cm = 36 cm.

Question 27: Arithmetic

Prompt: What is 50% of 200?

Answer: 100

Explanation: 50% of 200 is calculated as 0.50 × 200 = 100.

Question 28: Algebra

Prompt: If 3z - 9 = 0, what is the value of z?

Answer: 3

Explanation: Solve for z: 3z = 9. Then, divide both sides by 3: z = 9 / 3, which gives z = 3.

Question 29: Geometry

Prompt: A triangle has a base of 10 cm and a height of 6 cm. What is its area?

Answer: 30 cm²

Explanation: Area of a triangle = 1/2 × base × height. So, the area is 1/2 × 10 cm × 6 cm = 30 cm².

Question 30: Arithmetic

Prompt: Divide 180 by 6.

Answer: 30

Explanation: Dividing the numbers: 180 ÷ 6 = 30.

Question 31: Algebra

Prompt: Solve for y: 7y = 42.

Answer: 6

Explanation: Divide both sides by 7 to find y: y = 42 / 7, giving y = 6.

Question 32: Geometry

Prompt: The radius of a circle is 3 cm. What is its circumference? (Use π = 3.14)

Answer: Approximately 18.84 cm

Explanation: Circumference of a circle = $2\pi r$. So, the circumference is $2 \times 3.14 \times 3$ cm ≈ 18.84 cm.

Question 33: Arithmetic

Prompt: What is the difference between 500 and 123?

Answer: 377

Explanation: Subtracting the numbers: 500 - 123 = 377.

Question 34: Arithmetic

Prompt: Find the product of 25 and 4.

Answer: 100

Explanation: Multiplying the two numbers: 25 × 4 = 100.

Question 35: Algebra

Prompt: Solve for x in the equation: 10x = 50.

Answer: 5

Explanation: Divide both sides by 10 to solve for x: x = 50 / 10, giving x = 5.

Question 36: Geometry

Prompt: A rectangle has a length of 12 cm and a width of 5 cm. What is its area?

Answer: 60 cm²

Explanation: Area of a rectangle = length × width. So, the area is 12 cm × 5 cm = 60 cm².

Question 37: Arithmetic

Prompt: Subtract 150 from 350.

Answer: 200

Explanation: Subtracting the numbers: 350 - 150 = 200.

Question 38: Algebra

Prompt: If y - 3 = 4, what is the value of y?

Answer: 7

Explanation: Add 3 to both sides to solve for y: y = 4 + 3, which gives y = 7.

Question 39: Geometry

Prompt: What is the volume of a rectangular prism with length 8 cm, width 3 cm, and height 2 cm?

Answer: 48 cm³

Explanation: Volume of a rectangular prism = length × width × height. So, the volume is 8 cm × 3 cm × 2 cm = 48 cm³.

Question 40: Arithmetic

Prompt: What is 25% of 80?

Answer: 20

Explanation: 25% of 80 is calculated as $0.25 \times 80 = 20$.

Question 41: Algebra

Prompt: Solve for x: x/5 = 3.

Answer: 15

Explanation: Multiply both sides by 5 to solve for x: $x = 3 \times 5$, which gives $x = 15$.

Question 42: Geometry

Prompt: A circle has a diameter of 10 cm. What is its radius?

Answer: 5 cm

Explanation: Radius of a circle = diameter / 2. So, the radius is 10 cm / 2 = 5 cm.

Question 43: Arithmetic

Prompt: What is the sum of 456 and 321?

Answer: 777

Explanation: Adding the two numbers: 456 + 321 = 777.

Question 44: Arithmetic

Prompt: Calculate the sum of 98 and 75.

Answer: 173

Explanation: Adding the two numbers: 98 + 75 = 173.

Question 45: Algebra

Prompt: Solve for x in the equation: 4x + 8 = 24.

Answer: 4

Explanation: First, subtract 8 from both sides: $4x = 16$. Then, divide by 4: $x = 16 / 4$, giving $x = 4$.

Question 46: Geometry

Prompt: A square has a side length of 7 cm. What is its area?

Answer: 49 cm²

Explanation: Area of a square = side length². So, the area is 7 cm × 7 cm = 49 cm².

Question 47: Arithmetic

Prompt: Subtract 345 from 789.

Answer: 444

Explanation: Subtracting the numbers: 789 - 345 = 444.

Question 48: Algebra

Prompt: If y + 5 = 12, what is the value of y?

Answer: 7

Explanation: Subtract 5 from both sides to solve for y: y = 12 - 5, which gives y = 7.

Question 49: Geometry

Prompt: What is the perimeter of a rectangle with a length of 10 cm and a width of 6 cm?

Answer: 32 cm

Explanation: Perimeter of a rectangle = 2 × (length + width). So, the perimeter is 2 × (10 cm + 6 cm) = 32 cm.

Question 50: Arithmetic

Prompt: What is 30% of 200?

Answer: 60

Explanation: 30% of 200 is calculated as 0.30 × 200 = 60.

Question 51: Algebra

Prompt: Solve for x: 9x = 81.

Answer: 9

Explanation: Divide both sides by 9 to solve for x: x = 81 / 9, which gives x = 9.

Question 52: Geometry

Prompt: A triangle has a base of 6 cm and a height of 4 cm. What is its area?

Answer: 12 cm²

Explanation: Area of a triangle = 1/2 × base × height. So, the area is 1/2 × 6 cm × 4 cm = 12 cm².

Question 53: Arithmetic

Prompt: What is the result of 120 ÷ 4?

Answer: 30

Explanation: Dividing the numbers: 120 ÷ 4 = 30.

Question 54: Arithmetic

Prompt: Multiply 35 by 3.

Answer: 105

Explanation: Multiplying the numbers: 35 × 3 = 105.

Question 55: Algebra

Prompt: Solve for x in the equation: x/4 = 5.

Answer: 20

Explanation: Multiply both sides by 4 to solve for x: x = 5 × 4, giving x = 20.

Question 56: Geometry

Prompt: What is the area of a triangle with a base of 8 cm and a height of 5 cm?

Answer: 20 cm²

Explanation: Area of a triangle = 1/2 × base × height. So, the area is 1/2 × 8 cm × 5 cm = 20 cm².

Question 57: Arithmetic

Prompt: Subtract 234 from 567.

Answer: 333

Explanation: Subtracting the numbers: 567 - 234 = 333.

Question 58: Algebra

Prompt: If 6y - 18 = 12, what is the value of y?

Answer: 5

Explanation: Add 18 to both sides: 6y = 30. Then, divide by 6: y = 30 / 6, which gives y = 5.

Question 59: Geometry

Prompt: A circle has a radius of 6 cm. What is its circumference? (Use π = 3.14)

Answer: Approximately 37.68 cm

Explanation: Circumference of a circle = 2πr. So, the circumference is 2 × 3.14 × 6 cm ≈ 37.68 cm.

Question 60: Arithmetic

Prompt: What is 75% of 160?

Answer: 120

Explanation: 75% of 160 is calculated as 0.75 × 160 = 120.

Question 61: Algebra

Prompt: Solve for x: 5x + 15 = 40.

Answer: 5

Explanation: First, subtract 15 from both sides: $5x = 25$. Then, divide by 5: $x = 25 / 5$, giving $x = 5$.

Question 62: Geometry

Prompt: The perimeter of a square is 48 meters. What is the length of one side?

Answer: 12 meters

Explanation: Perimeter of a square = 4 × side length. So, one side equals the perimeter divided by 4: 48 meters / 4 = 12 meters.

Question 63: Arithmetic

Prompt: Divide 250 by 5.

Answer: 50

Explanation: Dividing the numbers: $250 \div 5 = 50$.

Question 64: Arithmetic

Prompt: What is the sum of 512 and 488?

Answer: 1000

Explanation: Adding the two numbers: 512 + 488 = 1000.

SECTION 5: LANGUAGE SKILLS

Question 1: Grammar

Prompt: Identify the error in the sentence: "Each of the students have completed their project on time."

A) Replace 'have' with 'has'
B) Replace 'their' with 'his or her'
C) No error
D) Replace 'Each' with 'All'

Answer: A) Replace 'have' with 'has'

Explanation: The subject 'Each of the students' is singular, so the verb should be singular as well ('has'). The correct sentence is: "Each of the students has completed their project on time."

Question 2: Punctuation

Prompt: Choose the correctly punctuated sentence:

A) After dinner, we decided to go for a walk.
B) After dinner we decided, to go for a walk.
C) After dinner we decided to go, for a walk.
D) After dinner, we decided to go for a walk.

Answer: A) After dinner, we decided to go for a walk.

Explanation: A comma should be used after an introductory phrase like 'After dinner'. The other options incorrectly place the comma, disrupting the natural flow of the sentence.

Question 3: Grammar

Prompt: Select the sentence that uses the correct verb tense:

A) He has written a letter to his friend yesterday.

B) He writes a letter to his friend yesterday.
C) He wrote a letter to his friend yesterday.
D) He had written a letter to his friend yesterday.

Answer: C) He wrote a letter to his friend yesterday.

Explanation: The correct verb tense for an action completed in the past (yesterday) is the simple past tense. 'Wrote' is the simple past tense of 'write', making option C correct.

Question 4: Punctuation

Prompt: Choose the sentence with the correct use of commas:

A) My brother, a doctor, will be moving to Boston soon.
B) My brother a doctor will be moving, to Boston soon.
C) My brother a doctor, will be moving to Boston soon.
D) My brother, a doctor will be moving to Boston soon.

Answer: A) My brother, a doctor, will be moving to Boston soon.

Explanation: Commas are used to set off appositives – words that rename or clarify a noun. 'A doctor' is an appositive that gives more information about 'My brother', hence it should be set off with commas.

Question 5: Grammar

Prompt: Identify the correct sentence:

  A) Neither the students nor the teacher was late for class.
  B) Neither the students nor the teacher were late for class.
  C) Neither the students or the teacher was late for class.
  D) Neither the students or the teacher were late for class.

Answer: A) Neither the students nor the teacher was late for class.

Question 6: Grammar

Prompt: Choose the sentence with correct subject-verb agreement:

A) The list of supplies were on the table.
B) The list of supplies was on the table.
C) The list of supplies are on the table.
D) The list of supplies be on the table.

Answer: B) The list of supplies was on the table.

Explanation: 'The list of supplies' is a singular subject, so it requires the singular verb 'was'. Option B correctly matches the subject with the singular verb.

Question 7: Punctuation

Prompt: Identify the sentence with correct comma usage:

  A) In the morning, I like to drink coffee, and read the newspaper.
  B) In the morning I like to drink coffee and read the newspaper.
  C) In the morning, I like to drink coffee and, read the newspaper.
  D) In the morning, I like to drink coffee, and read, the newspaper.

Answer: B) In the morning I like to drink coffee and read the newspaper.

Explanation: Option B is correct because it does not require a comma after 'morning'. The activities (drink coffee and read the newspaper) are part of a simple list that does not require a comma before the conjunction 'and'.

Question 8: Grammar

Prompt: Select the sentence that is grammatically correct:

  A) Me and my friend went to the movie last night.
  B) My friend and I went to the movie last night.
  C) I and my friend went to the movie last night.
  D) My friend and me went to the movie last night.

Answer: B) My friend and I went to the movie last night.

Explanation: When the subject of a sentence includes the speaker and another person, the correct form is 'My friend and I'. Option B correctly uses this form.

Question 9: Punctuation

Prompt: Choose the sentence that correctly uses semicolons:

A) We visited Berlin, it is a beautiful city; full of history.
B) We visited Berlin; it is a beautiful city full of history.
C) We visited; Berlin, it is a beautiful city; full of history.
D) We visited Berlin; it is a beautiful, city; full of history.

Answer: B) We visited Berlin; it is a beautiful city full of history.

Explanation: A semicolon is correctly used in option B to separate two closely related independent clauses.

Question 10: Grammar

Prompt: Identify the sentence with the correct plural form:

A) There are five mouses in the basement.
B) There are five mouse in the basement.
C) There are five mice in the basement.
D) There are five mices in the basement.

Answer: C) There are five mice in the basement.

Explanation: The correct plural form of 'mouse' is 'mice'. Option C uses the correct plural form.

Question 11: Grammar

Prompt: Choose the sentence that correctly uses comparative adjectives:

A) Of the two sisters, Jane is the more taller.
B) Of the two sisters, Jane is taller.
C) Of the two sisters, Jane is the tallest.
D) Of the two sisters, Jane is most tall.

Answer: B) Of the two sisters, Jane is taller.

Explanation: When comparing two items or people, the comparative form 'taller' is appropriate. Option B correctly uses 'taller' without the superlative 'the' or 'most'.

Question 12: Punctuation

Prompt: Identify the correctly punctuated sentence:

A) The teacher said, "Please open your books to page 20".

B) The teacher said "Please open your books to page 20."

C) The teacher said, "Please open your books to page 20."

D) The teacher said "Please open your books to page 20".

Answer: C) The teacher said, "Please open your books to page 20."

Explanation: In option C, the comma after 'said' correctly sets off the quoted speech, and the period is correctly placed inside the quotation marks at the end of the sentence.

Question 13: Grammar

Prompt: Select the sentence with correct pronoun usage:

A) Her and I went to the same school.
B) She and me went to the same school.
C) She and I went to the same school.
D) Her and me went to the same school.

Answer: C) She and I went to the same school.

Explanation: 'She and I' is the correct subject pronoun form for the sentence. Option C uses both pronouns correctly.

Question 14: Punctuation

Prompt: Choose the sentence with correct use of apostrophes:

  A) Its a sunny day in the Smiths' garden.
  B) It's a sunny day in the Smith's garden.
  C) Its a sunny day in the Smith's garden.
  D) It's a sunny day in the Smiths' garden.

Answer: D) It's a sunny day in the Smiths' garden.

Explanation: 'It's' is the contraction for 'it is', and 'Smiths" indicates possession by the Smith family (plural). Option D uses both apostrophes correctly.

Question 15: Grammar

Prompt: Identify the sentence with correct use of an adverb:

  A) She runs quick around the track.
  B) She runs quickly around the track.

C) She quickly runs around the track.
D) Both B and C are correct.

Answer: D) Both B and C are correct.

Explanation: Adverbs modify verbs, adjectives, or other adverbs. 'Quickly' is the adverb form of 'quick' and can be placed either before the verb ('quickly runs') or after the verb ('runs quickly'). Both options B and C use the adverb correctly.

Question 16: Grammar

Prompt: Identify the sentence with correct subject-verb agreement:

A) The committee have decided to postpone the event.
B) The committee has decided to postpone the event.
C) The committee are deciding to postpone the event.
D) The committee were deciding to postpone the event.

Answer: B) The committee has decided to postpone the event.

Explanation: 'The committee' is considered a singular collective noun and thus requires a singular verb. 'Has decided' is the correct form in this context.

Question 17: Punctuation

Prompt: Choose the sentence with correct punctuation:

   A) After considering all options, however, he decided not to travel.
   B) After considering all options however, he decided not to travel.
   C) After considering all options however; he decided not to travel.
   D) After considering all options, however; he decided not to travel.

Answer: A) After considering all options, however, he decided not to travel.

Explanation: Commas should be used around 'however' when it functions as a parenthetical element in the sentence. Option A uses commas correctly.

Question 18: Grammar

Prompt: Select the sentence that uses the correct plural form:

A) The children loves playing in the park.
B) The childrens love playing in the park.
C) The children love playing in the park.
D) The childs love playing in the park.

Answer: C) The children love playing in the park.

Explanation: 'Children' is the correct plural form of 'child', and with a plural subject, the verb should be 'love' not 'loves'. Option C is grammatically correct.

Question 19: Punctuation

Prompt: Identify the correctly punctuated sentence:

A) Before the movie started; we bought some popcorn.
B) Before the movie started, we bought some popcorn.
C) Before the movie, started we bought some popcorn.
D) Before the movie started we bought some popcorn.

Answer: B) Before the movie started, we bought some popcorn.

Explanation: A comma should be used after introductory phrases or clauses. Option B correctly places the comma after 'Before the movie started'.

Question 20: Grammar

Prompt: Choose the sentence with the correct use of the past perfect tense:

  A) She has finished her homework before dinner.
  B) She had finished her homework before dinner.
  C) She have finished her homework before dinner.
  D) She finishing her homework before dinner.

Answer: B) She had finished her homework before dinner.

Explanation: The past perfect tense ('had finished') is used to express an action completed before another past action. Option B correctly uses the past perfect tense to indicate that finishing homework occurred before dinner.

Question 21: Sentence Structure

Prompt: Identify the sentence with the correct structure:

   A) Although he was late for the meeting, but he still made a great impression.
   B) He still made a great impression although he was late for the meeting.
   C) He was late for the meeting, and he still made a great impression.
   D) Although he was late for the meeting, he still made a great impression.

Answer: D) Although he was late for the meeting, he still made a great impression.

Explanation: Option D correctly uses the subordinating conjunction 'Although' at the beginning of the sentence, followed by the main clause, without the unnecessary addition of 'but'.

Question 22: Sentence Structure

Prompt: Choose the sentence with correct parallel structure:

   A) She likes running, to swim, and biking.

B) She likes running, swimming, and biking.
C) She likes to run, swimming, and to bike.
D) She likes to run, swim, and biking.

Answer: B) She likes running, swimming, and biking.

Explanation: Option B maintains parallel structure by using gerunds ('running', 'swimming', 'biking') for all items in the list.

Question 23: Sentence Structure

Prompt: Identify the sentence with proper use of clauses:

A) Because he forgot his umbrella, and he got soaked in the rain.
B) He forgot his umbrella, and he got soaked in the rain.
C) Because he forgot his umbrella he got soaked in the rain.
D) He forgot his umbrella because he got soaked in the rain.

Answer: B) He forgot his umbrella, and he got soaked in the rain.

Explanation: Option B correctly uses a coordinating conjunction 'and' to connect two independent clauses, each of which could stand as a sentence on its own.

Question 24: Sentence Structure

Prompt: Select the sentence that correctly uses a complex sentence structure:

A) While she was reading, the phone rang.
B) She was reading and the phone rang.
C) She was reading the phone rang.
D) She was reading, the phone rang.

Answer: A) While she was reading, the phone rang.

Explanation: Option A correctly uses a complex sentence structure, combining an independent clause ('the phone rang') with a dependent clause ('While she was reading').

Question 25: Sentence Structure

Prompt: Choose the sentence that correctly avoids a run-on:

A) He ran fast he won the race.

B) He ran fast, he won the race.
C) He ran fast, and he won the race.
D) He ran fast; he won the race.

Answer: C) He ran fast, and he won the race.

Explanation: Option C correctly uses a comma and a coordinating conjunction 'and' to connect two independent clauses, avoiding a run-on sentence. Option D, with a semicolon, is also grammatically correct but C is more appropriate in this context.

Question 26: Sentence Structure

Prompt: Select the sentence with correct compound sentence structure:

A) After finishing her homework, she watched a movie, and she went to bed.
B) She finished her homework, watched a movie, and went to bed.
C) She finished her homework, and she watched a movie, and then she went to bed.
D) She finished her homework; she watched a movie, then she went to bed.

Answer: C) She finished her homework, and she watched a movie, and then she went to bed.

Explanation: Option C correctly uses a compound sentence structure with coordinating conjunctions 'and' to connect independent clauses.

Question 27: Sentence Structure

Prompt: Identify the sentence with the correct complex sentence structure:

  A) Although it was raining heavily, but they decided to go hiking.
  B) They decided to go hiking, although it was raining heavily.
  C) It was raining heavily they decided to go hiking.
  D) It was raining heavily, because they decided to go hiking.

Answer: B) They decided to go hiking, although it was raining heavily.

Explanation: Option B correctly uses a complex sentence structure, with 'Although it was raining heavily' as the dependent clause and 'they decided to go hiking' as the independent clause.

Question 28: Sentence Structure

Prompt: Choose the sentence that correctly avoids a sentence fragment:

   A) Because she was tired from the trip.
   B) She was tired from the trip.
   C) Tired from the trip, and she went to bed early.
   D) Was tired from the trip, she went to bed early.

Answer: B) She was tired from the trip.

Explanation: Option B is a complete sentence with a subject and a verb, providing a complete thought. The other options are fragments as they lack either a subject, verb, or complete thought.

Question 29: Sentence Structure

Prompt: Select the sentence with correct use of a subordinate clause:

   A) When she finishes her assignment, she will take a break.
   B) She finishes her assignment, and she will take a break.
   C) She finishes her assignment she will take a break.

D) Finishes her assignment, she will take a break.

Answer: A) When she finishes her assignment, she will take a break.

Explanation: Option A correctly uses a subordinate clause 'When she finishes her assignment' followed by the main clause 'she will take a break', creating a complex sentence.

Question 30: Sentence Structure

Prompt: Identify the sentence with proper use of coordinating conjunctions:

A) She wanted to go to the movies, but the tickets were sold out.
B) She wanted to go to the movies but, the tickets were sold out.
C) She wanted to go to the movies but the tickets, were sold out.
D) She wanted, to go to the movies but the tickets were sold out.

Answer: A) She wanted to go to the movies, but the tickets were sold out.

Explanation: Option A correctly uses the coordinating conjunction 'but' to connect two independent clauses, with the comma placed before 'but'.

Question 31: Sentence Structure

Prompt: Choose the sentence that correctly uses a dependent clause:

  A) Before she goes to the gym, she likes to eat a light snack.
  B) She likes to eat a light snack and goes to the gym.
  C) She likes to eat a light snack, goes to the gym.
  D) Likes to eat a light snack before she goes to the gym.

Answer: A) Before she goes to the gym, she likes to eat a light snack.

Explanation: Option A correctly uses the dependent clause 'Before she goes to the gym' at the beginning of the sentence, followed by the main clause 'she likes to eat a light snack', forming a complex sentence.

Question 32: Sentence Structure

Prompt: Identify the sentence with correct parallel structure:

A) She enjoys reading, to bake, and painting.
B) She enjoys reading, baking, and painting.
C) She enjoys to read, baking, and painting.
D) She enjoys reading, baking, and to paint.

Answer: B) She enjoys reading, baking, and painting.

Explanation: Option B maintains parallel structure by using gerunds ('reading', 'baking', 'painting') for all activities in the list.

Question 33: Sentence Structure

Prompt: Select the sentence with proper integration of an introductory phrase:

A) Without any doubt, the experiment was a success.
B) Without any doubt the experiment, was a success.
C) The experiment was a success without any doubt.

D) The experiment, without any doubt was a success.

Answer: A) Without any doubt, the experiment was a success.

Explanation: Option A correctly places a comma after the introductory phrase 'Without any doubt' before the main clause.

Question 34: Sentence Structure

Prompt: Choose the sentence that correctly avoids a comma splice:

A) She ran quickly, she still missed the bus.
B) She ran quickly; she still missed the bus.
C) She ran quickly, and she still missed the bus.
D) She ran quickly she still missed the bus.

Answer: C) She ran quickly, and she still missed the bus.

Explanation: Option C correctly uses a comma followed by the coordinating conjunction 'and' to connect two independent clauses, thus avoiding a comma splice.

Question 35: Sentence Structure

Prompt: Identify the sentence with correct use of a nonrestrictive element:

A) My brother, who is a doctor, will be moving to Boston.
B) My brother who is a doctor will be moving to Boston.
C) My brother who is a doctor, will be moving to Boston.
D) My brother, who is a doctor will be moving to Boston.

Answer: A) My brother, who is a doctor, will be moving to Boston.

Explanation: Option A correctly uses commas to set off the non-restrictive clause 'who is a doctor', which provides additional information about 'My brother' but is not essential to the meaning of the sentence.

Question 36: Sentence Structure

Prompt: Choose the sentence that correctly forms a compound sentence:

A) Although it was raining, she decided to walk to the store.

B) It was raining, but she decided to walk to the store.

C) It was raining she decided to walk to the store.

D) It was raining, she decided to walk to the store.

Answer: B) It was raining, but she decided to walk to the store.

Explanation: Option B correctly forms a compound sentence using a comma and the coordinating conjunction 'but' to connect two independent clauses.

Question 37: Sentence Structure

Prompt: Select the sentence with correct use of a participial phrase:

A) Walking to the store, the rain started to fall heavily.

B) The rain started to fall heavily, walking to the store.

C) Walking to the store, she felt the rain start to fall heavily.

D) She felt the rain start to fall heavily, walking to the store.

Answer: C) Walking to the store, she felt the rain start to fall heavily.

Explanation: Option C correctly places the participial phrase 'Walking to the store' at the beginning of the sentence, modifying the subject 'she'.

Question 38: Sentence Structure

Prompt: Identify the sentence with the correct use of a relative clause:

   A) The book that she read was on the table.
   B) The book she read it was on the table.
   C) The book, that she read, was on the table.
   D) The book it that she read was on the table.

Answer: A) The book that she read was on the table.

Explanation: Option A correctly uses the relative clause 'that she read' to provide additional information about 'The book'.

Question 39: Sentence Structure

Prompt: Choose the sentence with correct placement of modifiers:

A) She saw a kitten walking to the store.
B) Walking to the store, she saw a kitten.
C) She walking to the store saw a kitten.
D) She saw a kitten on her walk to the store.

Answer: B) Walking to the store, she saw a kitten.

Explanation: Option B correctly places the modifier 'Walking to the store' at the beginning of the sentence, indicating that 'she' was the one walking to the store.

Question 40: Sentence Structure

Prompt: Select the sentence with proper coordination of ideas:

A) He studied hard for the test, so he felt confident.
B) He studied hard for the test, he felt confident.
C) He studied hard for the test; he felt confident.
D) He studied hard for the test and felt confident.

Answer: A) He studied hard for the test, so he felt confident.

Explanation: Option A correctly uses the coordinating conjunction 'so' to connect two related ideas in a single sentence, indicating cause and effect.

Question 41: Spelling and Capitalization

Prompt: Choose the sentence with correct spelling and capitalization:

A) She visited the Eiffel Tower in paris last summer.
B) She visited the eiffel tower in Paris last Summer.
C) She visited the Eiffel Tower in Paris last summer.
D) She Visited the Eiffel tower in Paris Last summer.

Answer: C) She visited the Eiffel Tower in Paris last summer.

Explanation: 'Eiffel Tower' and 'Paris' are proper nouns and should be capitalized. 'Last summer' is correctly capitalized only at the beginning of the word 'Last'. Option C is correct in terms of both spelling and capitalization.

Question 42: Spelling and Capitalization

Prompt: Identify the sentence with correct spelling:

A) The archeologist made an exciting discovery.
B) The archeologyst made an exciting discovery.

C) The archaeologist made an exciting discovery.
D) The archaelogist made an exciting discovery.

Answer: C) The archaeologist made an exciting discovery.

Explanation: The correct spelling for the professional studying human history and prehistory is 'archaeologist'. Option C is spelled correctly.

Question 43: Spelling and Capitalization

Prompt: Choose the sentence with correct spelling and capitalization:

  A) Her favorite book is "To Kill a Mockingbird" by Harper Lee.
  B) Her favorite book is "to kill a Mockingbird" by Harper Lee.
  C) Her favorite book is "To Kill A Mockingbird" by Harper Lee.
  D) Her favorite book is "To Kill a Mockingbird" by harper Lee.

Answer: A) Her favorite book is "To Kill a Mockingbird" by Harper Lee.

Explanation: In the title 'To Kill a Mockingbird', all major words are capitalized, and 'a' being a preposition is not. The author's name, 'Harper Lee', is a proper noun and should be capitalized. Option A is correct.

Question 44: Spelling and Capitalization

Prompt: Identify the sentence with correct spelling:

A) We recieved an invitation to their wedding.
B) We received an invitation to their wedding.
C) We recieve an invitation to their wedding.
D) We receieved an invitation to their wedding.

Answer: B) We received an invitation to their wedding.

Explanation: The correct spelling is 'received'. The rule of 'i' before 'e' except after 'c' applies here. Option B is spelled correctly.

Question 45: Spelling and Capitalization

Prompt: Choose the sentence with correct spelling and capitalization:

A) In February, we often have alot of snow.

B) In february, we often have a lot of snow.
C) In February, we often have a lot of snow.
D) In February, we often have alot of snow.

Answer: C) In February, we often have a lot of snow.

Explanation: 'February' is a proper noun and should be capitalized. The phrase 'a lot' is two words, not 'alot'. Option C correctly uses both proper capitalization and spelling.

Question 46: Spelling and Capitalization

Prompt: Identify the sentence with correct spelling:

  A) The principle of the school announced a new policy.
  B) The principal of the school announced a new policy.
  C) The Principle of the school announced a new policy.
  D) The Principal of the school announced a new policy.

Answer: B) The principal of the school announced a new policy.

Explanation: 'Principal', referring to the head of a school, is the correct spelling. 'Principle' is a different word meaning a fundamental truth or proposition. Only 'principal' is correctly spelled and used in the context of this sentence.

Question 47: Spelling and Capitalization

Prompt: Choose the sentence with correct spelling and capitalization:

   A) The mississippi River is one of the longest rivers in the United States.
   B) The Mississippi river is one of the longest rivers in the United States.
   C) The Mississippi River is one of the longest rivers in the United States.
   D) The mississippi river is one of the longest rivers in the United States.

Answer: C) The Mississippi River is one of the longest rivers in the United States.

Explanation: 'Mississippi' and 'River' are proper nouns and should be capitalized. Option C correctly capitalizes both words.

Question 48: Spelling and Capitalization

Prompt: Identify the sentence with correct spelling:

  A) The weather forcast predicts rain tomorrow.
  B) The weather forecast predicts rain tomorrow.
  C) The weather forecst predicts rain tomorrow.
  D) The weather forcaste predicts rain tomorrow.

Answer: B) The weather forecast predicts rain tomorrow.

Explanation: The correct spelling is 'forecast', referring to a prediction or estimate of future events, especially concerning weather. Option B is spelled correctly.

Question 49: Spelling and Capitalization

Prompt: Choose the sentence with correct spelling and capitalization:

  A) We visited the Colosseum on our trip to Rome.
  B) We visited the colosseum on our trip to Rome.
  C) We visited the Colloseum on our trip to Rome.
  D) We visited the colosseum on our trip to rome.

Answer: A) We visited the Colosseum on our trip to Rome.

Explanation: 'Colosseum' is a proper noun referring to a specific historical landmark in Rome, and 'Rome' is the name of a city. Both should be capitalized. Option A correctly spells and capitalizes these nouns.

Question 50: Spelling and Capitalization

Prompt: Identify the sentence with correct spelling:

A) The accomodation was very comfortable.
B) The accommadation was very comfortable.
C) The accommodation was very comfortable.
D) The acommodation was very comfortable.

Answer: C) The accommodation was very comfortable.

Explanation: The correct spelling is 'accommodation', which refers to a place to stay or lodging. Option C is spelled correctly.

Question 51: Spelling and Capitalization

Prompt: Choose the sentence with correct spelling and capitalization:

A) My Aunt lives in San Francisco.
B) My aunt lives in San Francisco.
C) My Aunt lives in san Francisco.
D) My aunt lives in san francisco.

Answer: B) My aunt lives in San Francisco.

Explanation: 'Aunt' should not be capitalized unless used as part of a name, such as 'Aunt Mary'. 'San Francisco' is a proper noun and both words should be capitalized. Option B is correct.

Question 52: Spelling and Capitalization

Prompt: Identify the sentence with correct spelling:

A) She was greatful for the opportunity.
B) She was grateful for the opportunity.
C) She was greatfull for the opportunity.
D) She was gratefull for the opportunity.

Answer: B) She was grateful for the opportunity.

Explanation: The correct spelling is 'grateful', which means feeling or showing an appreciation for something. Option B is spelled correctly.

Question 53: Spelling and Capitalization

Prompt: Choose the sentence with correct spelling and capitalization:

A) The Declaration of Independance was a historic document.
B) The Declaration of Independence was a historic document.
C) The declaration of independence was a historic document.
D) The Declaration Of Independence Was A Historic Document.

Answer: B) The Declaration of Independence was a historic document.

Explanation: 'Declaration of Independence' is a proper noun referring to a specific historical document, and each major word should be capitalized. Option B correctly spells and capitalizes this term.

Question 54: Spelling and Capitalization

Prompt: Identify the sentence with correct spelling:

  A) The restraunt was known for its excellent cuisine.
  B) The restaurant was known for its excellent cuisine.
  C) The resturant was known for its excellent cuisine.
  D) The restaraunt was known for its excellent cuisine.

Answer: B) The restaurant was known for its excellent cuisine.

Explanation: The correct spelling is 'restaurant', which refers to a place where people pay to sit and eat meals. Option B is spelled correctly.

Question 55: Spelling and Capitalization

Prompt: Choose the sentence with correct spelling and capitalization:

  A) The children went to the museum on a field trip.
  B) The Children went to the Museum on a Field Trip.
  C) The children went to the Museum on a field trip.
  D) The children went to the museum on a Field Trip.

Answer: A) The children went to the museum on a field trip.

Explanation: Common nouns like 'children', 'museum', and 'field trip' should not be capitalized unless they are part of a proper noun or at the beginning of a sentence. Option A uses correct capitalization and spelling.

Question 56: Spelling and Capitalization

Prompt: Identify the sentence with correct spelling:

A) The scientist made a breakthru in his research.
B) The scientist made a breakthrough in his research.
C) The scientist made a breakthrew in his research.
D) The scientist made a breakthrought in his research.

Answer: B) The scientist made a breakthrough in his research.

Explanation: The correct spelling is 'breakthrough,' meaning a significant development or achievement. Option B is spelled correctly.

Question 57: Spelling and Capitalization

Prompt: Choose the sentence with correct spelling and capitalization:

  A) The Sahara desert is the largest hot desert in the world.
  B) The Sahara Desert is the largest hot desert in the world.
  C) The sahara desert is the largest hot desert in the world.
  D) The sahara Desert is the largest hot desert in the world.

Answer: B) The Sahara Desert is the largest hot desert in the world.

Explanation: 'Sahara' and 'Desert' are both part of a proper noun and should be capitalized. Option B correctly spells and capitalizes 'Sahara Desert.'

Question 58: Spelling and Capitalization

Prompt: Identify the sentence with correct spelling:

  A) He excells in playing the piano.
  B) He excels in playing the piano.
  C) He exells in playing the piano.

D) He excell's in playing the piano.

Answer: B) He excels in playing the piano.

Explanation: The correct spelling is 'excels,' meaning to be very good at or proficient in an activity or subject. Option B is spelled correctly.

Question 59: Spelling and Capitalization

Prompt: Choose the sentence with correct spelling and capitalization:

  A) The Magna carta is an important historical document.
  B) The Magna Carta is an important historical document.
  C) The magna Carta is an important historical document.
  D) The magna carta is an important historical document.

Answer: B) The Magna Carta is an important historical document.

Explanation: 'Magna Carta' is a proper noun and both words should be capitalized. Option B correctly spells and capitalizes 'Magna Carta.'

Question 60: Spelling and Capitalization

Prompt: Identify the sentence with correct spelling:

A) Her favourite color is blue.
B) Her favorite color is blue.
C) Her favorit color is blue.
D) Her favorate color is blue.

Answer: B) Her favorite color is blue.

Explanation: The correct American English spelling is 'favorite.' Option B is spelled correctly, while option A is the British English spelling.

Verbal Skills Section (100 questions)

Synonyms (25 questions):

1. Benevolent a) Kind b) Harsh c) Indifferent d) Selfish
2. Arduous a) Easy b) Difficult c) Simple d) Pleasant
3. Candid a) Dishonest b) Frank c) Secretive d) Vague
4. Diligent a) Lazy b) Careless c) Hardworking d) Inattentive
5. Eloquent a) Articulate b) Clumsy c) Silent d) Awkward
6. Frugal a) Wasteful b) Extravagant c) Economical d) Generous
7. Gregarious a) Solitary b) Unfriendly c) Sociable d) Shy
8. Harmony a) Discord b) Agreement c) Conflict d) Tension
9. Imperative a) Optional b) Crucial c) Unimportant d) Trivial
10. Jubilant a) Depressed b) Elated c) Angry d) Calm
11. Kinetic a) Static b) Motionless c) Dynamic d) Stable
12. Lucid a) Confused b) Clear c) Opaque d) Vague
13. Meticulous a) Careless b) Sloppy c) Precise d) Negligent
14. Novice a) Expert b) Beginner c) Master d) Professional

15. Obscure a) Clear b) Obvious c) Vague d) Apparent
16. Perseverance a) Quitting b) Laziness c) Endurance d) Surrender
17. Quandary a) Solution b) Dilemma c) Answer d) Clarity
18. Resilient a) Fragile b) Weak c) Flexible d) Brittle
19. Succinct a) Verbose b) Concise c) Long-winded d) Rambling
20. Tenacious a) Yielding b) Persistent c) Weak d) Feeble
21. Ubiquitous a) Rare b) Scarce c) Omnipresent d) Uncommon
22. Voracious a) Picky b) Ravenous c) Indifferent d) Apathetic
23. Wary a) Careless b) Cautious c) Reckless d) Naive
24. Xenophobia a) Tolerance b) Acceptance c) Fear of strangers d) Hospitality
25. Yield a) Resist b) Oppose c) Surrender d) Fight

Antonyms (25 questions):

26. Abundant a) Scarce b) Plentiful c) Ample d) Excessive
27. Benign a) Malignant b) Harmless c) Gentle d) Kind
28. Compassionate a) Cruel b) Empathetic c) Sympathetic d) Caring
29. Deter a) Encourage b) Discourage c) Prevent d) Hinder

30. Elated a) Depressed b) Joyful c) Excited d) Enthusiastic
31. Frugal a) Extravagant b) Thrifty c) Economical d) Miserly
32. Graceful a) Clumsy b) Elegant c) Refined d) Poised
33. Humble a) Arrogant b) Modest c) Meek d) Unassuming
34. Insipid a) Flavorful b) Bland c) Dull d) Boring
35. Jovial a) Melancholy b) Cheerful c) Merry d) Lighthearted
36. Knowledgeable a) Ignorant b) Informed c) Educated d) Wise
37. Lenient a) Strict b) Permissive c) Tolerant d) Indulgent
38. Magnanimous a) Petty b) Generous c) Noble d) Forgiving
39. Nonchalant a) Concerned b) Indifferent c) Apathetic d) Casual
40. Opaque a) Transparent b) Cloudy c) Obscure d) Dense
41. Prudent a) Reckless b) Cautious c) Wise d) Sensible
42. Quiescent a) Active b) Dormant c) Inactive d) Still
43. Repel a) Attract b) Repulse c) Deter d) Discourage
44. Spontaneous a) Planned b) Impulsive c) Impromptu d) Instinctive
45. Tarnish a) Polish b) Stain c) Dull d) Sully

46. Urbane a) Rustic b) Sophisticated c) Refined d) Polished

47. Vacillate a) Decide b) Waver c) Hesitate d) Fluctuate

48. Wane a) Increase b) Decline c) Diminish d) Fade

49. Xenophobic a) Welcoming b) Fearful c) Prejudiced d) Intolerant

Zealous a) Apathetic b) Enthusiastic c) Passionate d) FerventVerbal Analogies (25 questions):

51. CANVAS : PAINTER :: a) wood : carpenter b) string : violinist c) court : judge d) kitchen : chef

52. OASIS : DESERT :: a) island : ocean b) tree : forest c) star : galaxy d) book : library

53. DIPLOMA : GRADUATE :: a) paycheck : employee b) ticket : passenger c) key : homeowner d) license : driver

54. SIEVE : SEPARATE :: a) knife : cut b) broom : sweep c) hammer : build d) pen : write

55. MARATHON : ENDURANCE :: a) sprint : speed b) weightlifting : strength c) gymnastics : flexibility d) archery : precision

56. TURTLE : SHELL :: a) bird : feather b) fish : scale c) elephant : tusk d) snake : venom

57. PRESCRIPTION : DOCTOR :: a) verdict : judge b) sermon : priest c) lecture : professor d) speech : politician

58. APPLAUSE : APPROVAL :: a) laughter : humor b) tears : sadness c) shout : anger d) whisper : secrecy

59. FIRE : ASHES :: a) rain : puddles b) snow : slush
c) wind : breeze d) earthquake : rubble
60. APPRENTICE : MASTER :: a) student : teacher
b) child : parent c) employee : boss d) citizen :
government
61. SYMPTOM : DISEASE :: a) clue : mystery b)
chapter : book c) wave : ocean d) leaf : tree
62. PESSIMIST : OPTIMIST :: a) miser : spendthrift
b) introvert : extrovert c) pacifist : warmonger
d) amateur : professional
63. FLEDGLING : BIRD :: a) cub : bear b) kitten : cat
c) puppy : dog d) all of the above
64. ECLIPSE : SUN :: a) clouds : sky b) waves :
ocean c) leaves : tree d) curtains : window
65. DIRECTOR : FILM :: a) author : book b) chef :
meal c) architect : building d) all of the above
66. MONOPOLY : COMPETITION :: a) democracy :
dictatorship b) peace : war c) friendship : rivalry
d) knowledge : ignorance
67. MEDICINE : ILLNESS :: a) food : hunger b)
water : thirst c) sleep : fatigue d) all of the
above
68. VENOMOUS : SNAKE :: a) prickly : cactus b)
fast : cheetah c) tall : giraffe d) all of the above
69. LIGHT : PHOTON :: a) sound : wave b) heat :
molecule c) electricity : electron d) gravity :
mass
70. GALLERY : ART :: a) library : books b) stadium :
sports c) theater : plays d) all of the above

71. HARVEST : CROP :: a) mining : ore b) fishing : catch c) logging : timber d) all of the above

72. FAMINE : FOOD :: a) drought : water b) poverty : money c) illiteracy : education d) all of the above

73. SEISMOGRAPH : EARTHQUAKE :: a) thermometer : temperature b) barometer : pressure c) anemometer : wind d) all of the above

74. PACIFIST : WAR :: a) vegetarian : meat b) teetotaler : alcohol c) atheist : religion d) all of the above

75. OPAQUE : TRANSPARENT :: a) solid : liquid b) rough : smooth c) dull : shiny d) all of the above

Word Classification (25 questions):

76. Which word does not belong? a) Hammer b) Screwdriver c) Wrench d) Paintbrush

77. Which word does not belong? a) Oak b) Maple c) Pine d) Daisy

78. Which word does not belong? a) Soccer b) Basketball c) Tennis d) Chess

79. Which word does not belong? a) Violin b) Piano c) Trumpet d) Easel

80. Which word does not belong? a) Mercury b) Venus c) Mars d) Moon

81. Which word does not belong? a) Novel b) Poem c) Essay d) Pencil

82. Which word does not belong? a) Lion b) Tiger c) Elephant d) Crocodile

83. Which word does not belong? a) Carrot b) Potato c) Turnip d) Lettuce
84. Which word does not belong? a) Copper b) Silver c) Gold d) Silk
85. Which word does not belong? a) Sedan b) Truck c) Motorcycle d) Airplane
86. Which word does not belong? a) Shirt b) Pants c) Socks d) Umbrella
87. Which word does not belong? a) Dolphin b) Shark c) Whale d) Octopus
88. Which word does not belong? a) Diamond b) Ruby c) Emerald d) Crystal
89. Which word does not belong? a) Celsius b) Fahrenheit c) Kelvin d) Pound
90. Which word does not belong? a) Democracy b) Monarchy c) Oligarchy d) Liberty
91. Which word does not belong? a) Painting b) Sculpture c) Photography d) Literature
92. Which word does not belong? a) Oxygen b) Hydrogen c) Nitrogen d) Water
93. Which word does not belong? a) Apple b) Banana c) Orange d) Potato
94. Which word does not belong? a) Liver b) Heart c) Kidney d) Stomach
95. Which word does not belong? a) Comedy b) Tragedy c) Drama d) Actor
96. Which word does not belong? a) Square b) Triangle c) Circle d) Cube
97. Which word does not belong? a) Inch b) Foot c) Yard d) Gallon

98. Which word does not belong? a) Flu b) Pneumonia c) Diabetes d) Fracture
99. Which word does not belong? a) Trombone b) Clarinet c) Flute d) Guitar
100. Which word does not belong? a) Cotton b) Wool c) Silk d) Leather

Quantitative Skills Section (100 questions)

Number Series (40 questions):

101. What is the next number in the series? 2, 4, 6, 8, ___ a) 9 b) 10 c) 11 d) 12
102. What is the next number in the series? 1, 3, 6, 10, ___ a) 13 b) 14 c) 15 d) 16
103. What is the next number in the series? 3, 6, 12, 24, ___ a) 36 b) 42 c) 48 d) 54
104. What is the next number in the series? 1, 4, 9, 16, ___ a) 20 b) 23 c) 25 d) 28
105. What is the next number in the series? 2, 5, 10, 17, ___ a) 24 b) 26 c) 28 d) 30
106. What is the next number in the series? 1, 1, 2, 3, 5, ___ a) 7 b) 8 c) 9 d) 10
107. What is the next number in the series? 3, 7, 15, 31, ___ a) 47 b) 57 c) 63 d) 67
108. What is the next number in the series? 2, 6, 12, 20, ___ a) 28 b) 30 c) 32 d) 34
109. What is the next number in the series? 5, 10, 20, 35, ___ a) 50 b) 55 c) 60 d) 65
110. What is the next number in the series? 1, 3, 7, 15, ___ a) 23 b) 27 c) 31 d) 35
111. What is the next number in the series? 4, 7, 12, 19, ___ a) 26 b) 28 c) 30 d) 32

112.   What is the next number in the series? 2, 4, 8, 16, ___ a) 24 b) 28 c) 32 d) 36

113.   What is the next number in the series? 1, 5, 13, 25, ___ a) 37 b) 41 c) 45 d) 49

114.   What is the next number in the series? 3, 6, 11, 18, ___ a) 25 b) 27 c) 29 d) 31

115.   What is the next number in the series? 2, 5, 11, 23, ___ a) 35 b) 41 c) 47 d) 53

116.   What is the next number in the series? 1, 2, 4, 7, 11, ___ a) 15 b) 16 c) 17 d) 18

117.   What is the next number in the series? 3, 8, 15, 24, ___ a) 33 b) 35 c) 37 d) 39

118.   What is the next number in the series? 4, 9, 16, 25, ___ a) 34 b) 36 c) 38 d) 40

119.   What is the next number in the series? 2, 6, 18, 54, ___ a) 108 b) 126 c) 150 d) 162

120.   What is the next number in the series? 5, 8, 13, 21, ___ a) 29 b) 32 c) 34 d) 37

121.   What is the next number in the series? 1, 4, 10, 22, ___ a) 36 b) 40 c) 46 d) 52

122.   What is the next number in the series? 3, 5, 9, 17, ___ a) 27 b) 31 c) 33 d) 35

123.   What is the next number in the series? 2, 7, 14, 23, ___ a) 32 b) 34 c) 36 d) 38

124.   What is the next number in the series? 1, 3, 8, 19, ___ a) 36 b) 42 c) 46 d) 50

125.   What is the next number in the series? 4, 6, 10, 18, ___ a) 28 b) 30 c) 32 d) 34

126.   What is the next number in the series? 2, 5, 9, 14, ___ a) 18 b) 20 c) 22 d) 24

127. What is the next number in the series? 3, 7, 13, 21, ___ a) 29 b) 31 c) 33 d) 35

128. What is the next number in the series? 1, 6, 15, 28, ___ a) 41 b) 43 c) 45 d) 47

129. What is the next number in the series? 5, 11, 19, 29, ___ a) 39 b) 41 c) 43 d) 45

130. What is the next number in the series? 2, 8, 18, 32, ___ a) 48 b) 50 c) 52 d) 54

131. What is the next number in the series? 1, 5, 14, 30, ___ a) 51 b) 53 c) 55 d) 57

132. What is the next number in the series? 3, 9, 19, 33, ___ a) 49 b) 51 c) 53 d) 55

133. What is the next number in the series? 4, 10, 22, 46, ___ a) 92 b) 94 c) 96 d) 98

134. What is the next number in the series? 2, 6, 13, 23, ___ a) 34 b) 36 c) 38 d) 40

135. What is the next number in the series? 1, 4, 11, 26, ___ a) 55 b) 57 c) 59 d) 61

136. What is the next number in the series? 5, 12, 23, 38, ___ a) 55 b) 57 c) 59 d) 61

137. What is the next number in the series? 3, 8, 17, 32, ___ a) 51 b) 53 c) 55 d) 57

138. What is the next number in the series? 2, 7, 16, 31, ___ a) 50 b) 52 c) 54 d) 56

139. What is the next number in the series? 1, 5, 13, 27, ___ a) 45 b) 47 c) 49 d) 51

140. What is the next number in the series? 4, 11, 22, 37, ___ a) 54 b) 56 c) 58 d) 60

Certainly, I'll continue with the Geometric Comparisons subsection and then move on to the Non-geometric Comparisons subsection to complete the Quantitative Skills section.

Geometric Comparisons (30 questions):

141. Which shape has the most sides? a) Triangle b) Pentagon c) Octagon d) Hexagon

142. If a square has a side length of 5 cm, what is its area? a) 20 cm² b) 25 cm² c) 30 cm² d) 35 cm²

143. Which of the following is not a type of triangle? a) Isosceles b) Scalene c) Equilateral d) Parallelogram

144. What is the sum of the interior angles of a triangle? a) 90° b) 180° c) 270° d) 360°

145. If a rectangle has a length of 8 cm and a width of 5 cm, what is its perimeter? a) 13 cm b) 26 cm c) 40 cm d) 52 cm

146. Which of these shapes is not a quadrilateral? a) Rectangle b) Rhombus c) Trapezoid d) Pentagon

147. What is the formula for the area of a circle? a) πr b) 2πr c) πr² d) 2πr²

148. How many faces does a cube have? a) 4 b) 6 c) 8 d) 12

149. What is the measure of each interior angle in a regular pentagon? a) 72° b) 108° c) 120° d) 144°

150. If a triangle has a base of 6 cm and a height of 4 cm, what is its area? a) 10 cm² b) 12 cm² c) 14 cm² d) 16 cm²

151. Which of these 3D shapes has the most faces? a) Cube b) Tetrahedron c) Octahedron d) Dodecahedron

152. What is the formula for the volume of a sphere? a) $4/3\pi r^2$ b) $4/3\pi r^3$ c) $1/3\pi r^2 h$ d) $\pi r^2 h$

153. In a right triangle, what is the name of the side opposite the right angle? a) Adjacent b) Opposite c) Hypotenuse d) Base

154. What is the measure of each interior angle in a regular hexagon? a) 90° b) 108° c) 120° d) 135°

155. If a cylinder has a radius of 3 cm and a height of 5 cm, what is its volume? a) 45π cm³ b) 30π cm³ c) 15π cm³ d) 60π cm³

156. Which of these is not a type of quadrilateral? a) Square b) Rhombus c) Trapezoid d) Octagon

157. What is the formula for the area of a trapezoid? a) bh b) 1/2bh c) (a+b)h d) 1/2(a+b)h

158. How many vertices does a cube have? a) 4 b) 6 c) 8 d) 12

159. What is the name of a triangle with two equal sides? a) Equilateral b) Isosceles c) Scalene d) Right

160.   If a square has a diagonal of 10 cm, what is the length of its side? a) 5 cm b) 5√2 cm c) 10 cm d) 10√2 cm

161.   What is the formula for the surface area of a sphere? a) $4\pi r$ b) $4\pi r^2$ c) $4/3\pi r^3$ d) $2\pi r^2$

162.   In a right triangle, what is the relationship between the sides according to the Pythagorean theorem? a) $a^2 + b^2 = c^2$ b) $a + b = c$ c) $a^2 - b^2 = c^2$ d) $(a+b)^2 = c^2$

163.   What is the measure of each exterior angle in a regular octagon? a) 45° b) 60° c) 135° d) 225°

164.   If a rectangular prism has a length of 5 cm, width of 3 cm, and height of 4 cm, what is its volume? a) 12 cm³ b) 30 cm³ c) 60 cm³ d) 120 cm³

165.   What is the name of a quadrilateral with only one pair of parallel sides? a) Parallelogram b) Rectangle c) Trapezoid d) Rhombus

166.   How many diagonals does a pentagon have? a) 2 b) 3 c) 4 d) 5

167.   What is the formula for the area of a parallelogram? a) lw b) bh c) 1/2bh d) πr^2

168.   If a circle has a diameter of 10 cm, what is its circumference? a) 5π cm b) 10π cm c) 20π cm d) 25π cm

169.   What is the name of the line segment that connects the center of a circle to any point

on its circumference? a) Diameter b) Chord c) Tangent d) Radius

170. In a 30-60-90 triangle, if the shortest side is 5 cm, what is the length of the hypotenuse? a) 5√2 cm b) 5√3 cm c) 10 cm d) 10√3 cm

Non-geometric Comparisons (30 questions):

171. If 3x + 5 = 20, what is the value of x? a) 3 b) 5 c) 7 d) 15

172. Which of these fractions is the largest? a) 3/4 b) 2/3 c) 5/8 d) 7/10

173. If a car travels 240 miles in 4 hours, what is its average speed? a) 40 mph b) 50 mph c) 60 mph d) 70 mph

174. What is 25% of 80? a) 15 b) 20 c) 25 d) 30

175. If 5 apples cost 2,howmuchwould12applescost?a)2,howmuchwould12applescost?a)3.60 b) 4.20c)4.20c)4.80 d) $5.40

176. What is the next prime number after 17? a) 18 b) 19 c) 21 d) 23

177. If x² = 49, what are the possible values of x? a) 7 only b) -7 only c) Both 7 and -7 d) Neither 7 nor -7

178. What is the least common multiple of 6 and 8? a) 12 b) 24 c) 36 d) 48

179. If 3y - 2 = 13, what is the value of y? a) 3 b) 4 c) 5 d) 6

180. Which of these numbers is not a factor of 24? a) 3 b) 4 c) 5 d) 6

181. If a recipe calls for 3/4 cup of sugar and you want to double the recipe, how much sugar do you need? a) 1 cup b) 1 1/4 cups c) 1 1/2 cups d) 2 cups

182. What is the value of $2^3 \times 2^4$? a) 2^7 b) 2^{12} c) 4^7 d) 8^7

183. If $4x + 3 = 19$, what is the value of $2x$? a) 4 b) 6 c) 8 d) 10

184. What is the square root of 144? a) 10 b) 11 c) 12 d) 14

185. If a box contains 5 red marbles, 3 blue marbles, and 2 green marbles, what is the probability of drawing a blue marble? a) 1/5 b) 3/10 c) 2/5 d) 1/2

186. What is the result of 0.25×0.75? a) 0.1875 b) 0.2875 c) 0.3875 d) 0.4875

187. If $2y + 5 = 17$, what is the value of $y + 3$? a) 6 b) 7 c) 8 d) 9

188. What is the greatest common factor of 18 and 24? a) 3 b) 6 c) 9 d) 12

189. If a triangle has angles measuring 30° and 60°, what is the measure of the third angle? a) 60° b) 90° c) 120° d) 180°

190. What is the value of 5! (5 factorial)? a) 60 b) 90 c) 120 d) 150

191. If $3a = 21$, what is the value of $a/2$? a) 3 b) 3.5 c) 4 d) 4.5

192. What is the result of $(-3)^2 + 4^2$? a) 7 b) 16 c) 25 d) 34

193. If $8x - 3 = 29$, what is the value of $4x$? a) 14 b) 16 c) 18 d) 20

194. What is the median of the numbers 3, 7, 8, 12, 15? a) 7 b) 8 c) 9 d) 12

195. If a rectangle's length is twice its width and its perimeter is 30 cm, what is its width? a) 4 cm b) 5 cm c) 6 cm d) 7 cm

196. What is the value of $\sqrt{36} + \sqrt{64}$? a) 10 b) 12 c) 14 d) 16

197. If 2/3 of a number is 18, what is the number? a) 24 b) 26 c) 27 d) 30

198. What is the result of 3.5×0.2? a) 0.07 b) 0.7 c) 7 d) 70

199. If $5x + 2y = 22$ and $2x + y = 10$, what is the value of x? a) 2 b) 3 c) 4 d) 5

What is the sum of the first 10 positive integers? a) 45 b) 50 c) 55 d) 60Reading Comprehension Section (50 questions)

For this section, I'll provide short passages followed by questions about each passage. Let's begin:

Passage 1: The Industrial Revolution, which began in Britain in the late 18th century, was a period of great technological innovation and social change. It marked a major turning point in history, influencing almost every aspect of daily life. The transition included going from hand production methods to machines, new chemical manufacturing and iron production processes, improved efficiency of water power, the increasing use of steam power, and the development of machine tools. It also included the change from wood and other bio-fuels to coal.

201.   When did the Industrial Revolution begin? a) Early 17th century b) Mid 18th century c) Late 18th century d) Early 19th century

202.   Which of the following was NOT mentioned as a change during the Industrial Revolution? a) Increased use of machine tools b) Improved efficiency of water power c) Development of nuclear power d) New chemical manufacturing processes

203.   What fuel source became more prominent during the Industrial Revolution? a) Wood b) Coal c) Oil d) Natural gas

204.   The passage suggests that the Industrial Revolution: a) Only affected manufacturing processes b) Had little impact on daily life c) Influenced almost every aspect of daily life d) Was confined to Britain

205.   Which of the following best describes the transition in production methods? a) From machines to hand production b) From hand production to machines c) From steam power to water power d) From coal to bio-fuels

Passage 2: Photosynthesis is a process used by plants and other organisms to convert light energy into chemical energy that can later be released to fuel the organisms' activities. This chemical energy is stored in carbohydrate molecules, such as sugars, which are synthesized from carbon dioxide and water. Oxygen is released as a byproduct. Most plants, algae, and cyanobacteria perform photosynthesis; such organisms are called photoautotrophs. Photosynthesis is largely responsible for producing and maintaining the oxygen content of the Earth's atmosphere, and supplies most of the energy necessary for life on Earth.

206. What is the main purpose of photosynthesis? a) To release oxygen b) To convert chemical energy into light energy c) To convert light energy into chemical energy d) To absorb carbon dioxide from the atmosphere

207. Which of the following is NOT mentioned as a product of photosynthesis? a) Oxygen b) Carbohydrates c) Sugars d) Proteins

208. What are organisms that perform photosynthesis called? a) Heterotrophs b) Autotrophs c) Photoautotrophs d) Chemotrophs

209. According to the passage, what is one of the significant impacts of photosynthesis on Earth? a) It depletes the ozone layer b) It maintains the oxygen content of the atmosphere c) It increases global warming d) It reduces biodiversity

210. Which of the following is NOT mentioned as a raw material for

photosynthesis? a) Light b) Carbon dioxide c) Water d) Nitrogen

Passage 3: The American Civil War was a civil war in the United States fought from 1861 to 1865. The Union faced secessionists in eleven Southern states grouped together as the Confederate States of America. The Civil War began primarily as a result of the long-standing controversy over the enslavement of black people. War broke out in April 1861 when secessionist forces attacked Fort Sumter in South Carolina, just over a month after Abraham Lincoln had been inaugurated as the President of the United States. The loyalists of the Union in the North, which also included some geographically western and southern states, proclaimed support for the Constitution. They faced secessionists of the Confederate States in the South, who advocated for states' rights to uphold slavery.

211. What was the primary cause of the American Civil War? a) Economic disputes between states b) Controversy over the enslavement of black people c) Disagreements over foreign policy d) Religious conflicts

212. When did the Civil War begin? a) March 1861 b) April 1861 c) May 1861 d) June 1861

213. How many Southern states formed the Confederate States of America? a) 9 b) 10 c) 11 d) 13

214. What event marked the beginning of the Civil War? a) The inauguration of Abraham

Lincoln b) The attack on Fort Sumter c) The secession of South Carolina d) The Emancipation Proclamation

What did the secessionists in the South advocate for? a) Abolition of slavery b) States' rights to uphold slavery c) A stronger federal government d) Economic reformsPassage 4: The human brain is the central organ of the human nervous system, and with the spinal cord makes up the central nervous system. The brain consists of the cerebrum, the brainstem and the cerebellum. It controls most of the activities of the body, processing, integrating, and coordinating the information it receives from the sense organs, and making decisions as to the instructions sent to the rest of the body. The brain is contained in, and protected by, the skull bones of the head. The cerebrum is the largest part of the human brain. It is divided into two cerebral hemispheres. The cerebral cortex is an outer layer of grey matter, covering the core of white matter. The cortex is split into the neocortex and the much smaller allocortex. The neocortex is made up of six neuronal layers, while the allocortex has three or four. Each hemisphere is conventionally divided into four lobes – the frontal, temporal, parietal, and occipital lobes.

216.   What are the three main parts of the brain mentioned in the passage? a) Cerebrum, brainstem, and medulla b) Cerebrum, brainstem, and cerebellum c) Cerebrum, cortex,

and cerebellum d) Neocortex, allocortex, and brainstem

217. What protects the brain? a) The spinal cord b) The skull bones c) The cerebral cortex d) The white matter

218. Which is the largest part of the human brain? a) Cerebellum b) Brainstem c) Cerebrum d) Neocortex

219. How many neuronal layers does the neocortex have? a) Three b) Four c) Five d) Six

220. How many lobes is each cerebral hemisphere conventionally divided into? a) Two b) Three c) Four d) Six

Passage 5: Climate change is a long-term change in the average weather patterns that have come to define Earth's local, regional and global climates. These changes have a broad range of observed effects that are synonymous with the term. Changes observed in Earth's climate since the early 20th century are primarily driven by human activities, particularly fossil fuel burning, which increases heat-trapping greenhouse gas levels in Earth's atmosphere, raising Earth's average surface temperature. These human-produced temperature increases are commonly referred to as global warming. Natural processes can also contribute to climate change, including internal variability (e.g., cyclical ocean patterns like El Niño, La Niña and the Pacific Decadal Oscillation) and external forcings (e.g., volcanic activity, changes in the Sun's energy output, variations in Earth's orbit).

221.   What is the primary driver of climate change since the early 20th century? a) Natural processes b) Volcanic activity c) Human activities d) Changes in Earth's orbit

222.   Which human activity is specifically mentioned as contributing to climate change? a) Deforestation b) Fossil fuel burning c) Agriculture d) Urbanization

223.   What term is commonly used to refer to human-produced temperature increases? a) Climate variation b) Global warming c) Greenhouse effect d) Atmospheric change

224.   Which of the following is NOT mentioned as a natural process contributing to climate change? a) El Niño b) Volcanic activity c) Earth's orbital variations d) Plate tectonics

225.   According to the passage, what does burning fossil fuels increase in Earth's atmosphere? a) Oxygen levels b) Ozone levels c) Nitrogen levels d) Greenhouse gas levels

This concludes the Reading Comprehension section. Now, let's move on to the Language Skills section.

Language Skills Section (50 questions)

This section will test your knowledge of grammar, punctuation, and sentence structure.

226.   Choose the correct form of the verb: The team _____ to practice every day. a) have b) has c) are d) is

227. Identify the grammatically correct sentence: a) Neither of the students were prepared for the test. b) Neither of the students was prepared for the test. c) Neither of the student was prepared for the test. d) Neither of the students weren't prepared for the test.

228. Select the correct punctuation: The restaurant offers three desserts chocolate cake ice cream and fruit salad. a) The restaurant offers three desserts: chocolate cake, ice cream, and fruit salad. b) The restaurant offers three desserts, chocolate cake, ice cream and fruit salad. c) The restaurant offers three desserts: chocolate cake ice cream and fruit salad. d) The restaurant offers three desserts; chocolate cake, ice cream, and fruit salad.

229. Choose the correct pronoun: It was _____ who completed the project on time. a) I b) me c) myself d) mine

230. Identify the sentence with correct subject-verb agreement: a) The quality of the apples were excellent. b) The quality of the apples was excellent. c) The quality of the apples have been excellent. d) The quality of the apples are excellent.

231. Select the correctly spelled word: a) accomodate b) acommodate c) accommodate d) accomadate

232. Choose the correct form of the adjective: This is the _____ day of my life. a) good b) better c) best d) most good

233. Identify the sentence with correct parallel structure: a) He likes swimming, to hike, and riding bicycles. b) He likes swimming, hiking, and riding bicycles. c) He likes to swim, hiking, and to ride bicycles. d) He likes to swim, to hike, and riding bicycles.

234. Select the correct verb tense: By the time we arrive, the movie _____. a) will start b) will have started c) has started d) is starting

236. Choose the correct preposition: The cat jumped _____ the table. a) on b) in c) at d) byIdentify the sentence with correct use of apostrophes: a) The dogs' bowl is empty. b) The dog's bowls' are empty. c) The dogs bowls are empty. d) The dog's bowl's are empty.

237. Choose the correct form of the adverb: She sang the national anthem _____. a) beautiful b) more beautiful c) beautifully d) most beautiful

238. Select the sentence with correct capitalization: a) We visited new York city last Summer. b) We visited New york City last summer. c) We visited New York City last summer. d) We visited new York City last Summer.

239. Identify the correct use of who/whom: _____ did you give the book to? a) Who b) Whom c) Whose d) Which

240. Choose the correct conjunctive adverb: It was raining; _____, we decided to stay indoors. a) therefore b) however c) moreover d) furthermore

241. Select the sentence with correct subject-verb agreement: a) Either of the two options are acceptable. b) Either of the two options is acceptable. c) Either of the two options have been acceptable. d) Either of the two options were acceptable.

242. Identify the correctly punctuated sentence: a) "Where are you going?" She asked. b) "Where are you going," she asked? c) "Where are you going?" she asked. d) "Where are you going"? She asked.

243. Choose the correct form of the comparative adjective: This building is _____ than the one next door. a) more taller b) tallest c) more tall d) taller

244. Select the sentence with correct use of commas: a) After finishing his homework John went to the park. b) After finishing his homework, John went to the park. c) After finishing his homework John, went to the park. d) After finishing his homework, John, went to the park.

245.   Identify the correct use of lay/lie: Please _____ the book on the table. a) lay b) lie c) lain d) laid

246.   Choose the correct form of the verb: If I _____ rich, I would travel the world. a) am b) was c) were d) be

247.   Select the sentence with correct use of semicolons: a) I have three pets; a dog, a cat; and a fish. b) I have three pets: a dog; a cat; and a fish. c) I have three pets; a dog, a cat, and a fish. d) I have three pets; a dog; a cat; and a fish.

248.   Identify the correct use of affect/effect: The new policy will _____ everyone in the company. a) affect b) effect c) affected d) effected

249.   Choose the correct pronoun: Between you and _____, I think the test was quite difficult. a) I b) me c) myself d) mine

Select the sentence with correct subject-verb agreement: a) The news are good today. b) The news is good today. c) The news have been good today. d) The news were good today. This section will test your vocabulary, word relationships, and verbal reasoning skills.

251.   Choose the word that best completes the sentence: The detective's _____ skills helped him solve the mystery quickly. a) astute b) obtuse c) abstruse d) recondite

252. Select the pair of words with the relationship most similar to: CANVAS : PAINTER a) wood : carpenter b) pen : author c) stage : actor d) clay : sculptor

253. Identify the word that is closest in meaning to "benevolent": a) malicious b) charitable c) indifferent d) hostile

254. Choose the word that is opposite in meaning to "frugal": a) economical b) thrifty c) extravagant d) prudent

256. Select the word that does not belong in the group: a) pine b) oak c) maple d) daisyChoose the word that best completes the analogy: SYMPHONY : COMPOSER :: NOVEL : _____ a) Reader b) Writer c) Editor d) Publisher

257. Identify the word with the closest meaning to "ephemeral": a) Eternal b) Transient c) Substantial d) Permanent

258. Select the pair of words with the relationship most similar to: OASIS : DESERT a) Island : Ocean b) Mountain : Valley c) River : Forest d) City : Country

259. Choose the word that is opposite in meaning to "verbose": a) Concise b) Loquacious c) Garrulous d) Talkative

260. Identify the word that does not belong in the group: a) Courageous b) Intrepid c) Valiant d) Timorous

261. Select the word that best completes the sentence: The politician's _____ remarks

offended many of his constituents. a) diplomatic b) tactful c) insensitive d) judicious

262. Choose the word with the closest meaning to "ubiquitous": a) Rare b) Omnipresent c) Scarce d) Unusual

263. Identify the pair of words with the relationship most similar to: DIRECTOR : FILM a) Author : Book b) Artist : Painting c) Conductor : Orchestra d) Chef : Restaurant

264. Select the word that is opposite in meaning to "opaque": a) Transparent b) Cloudy c) Dense d) Obscure

265. Choose the word that does not belong in the group: a) Ecstatic b) Elated c) Jubilant d) Melancholy

266. Identify the word that best completes the sentence: The scientist's _____ research led to a groundbreaking discovery. a) superficial b) meticulous c) careless d) haphazard

267. Select the pair of words with the relationship most similar to: ANACHRONISM : TIME a) Anomaly : Conformity b) Synonym : Meaning c) Analogy : Comparison d) Antonym : Opposite

268. Choose the word with the closest meaning to "surreptitious": a) Open b) Clandestine c) Obvious d) Apparent

269. Identify the word that is opposite in meaning to "benign": a) Gentle b) Harmless c) Malignant d) Favorable

270. Select the word that does not belong in the group: a) Gregarious b) Sociable c) Outgoing d) Reticent

271. Choose the word that best completes the analogy: CARTOGRAPHER : MAP :: LEXICOGRAPHER : _____ a) Book b) Dictionary c) Atlas d) Encyclopedia

272. Identify the word with the closest meaning to "laconic": a) Verbose b) Terse c) Loquacious d) Garrulous

273. Select the pair of words with the relationship most similar to: ZENITH : NADIR a) Top : Bottom b) East : West c) North : South d) Left : Right

274. Choose the word that is opposite in meaning to "lucid": a) Clear b) Obscure c) Transparent d) Intelligible

275. Identify the word that does not belong in the group: a) Diligent b) Industrious c) Assiduous d) Indolent

276. Select the word that best completes the sentence: The journalist's _____ reporting exposed the corruption within the government. a) biased b) impartial c) prejudiced d) partial

277. Choose the word with the closest meaning to "quintessential": a) Typical b) Unusual c) Rare d) Uncommon

278. Identify the pair of words with the relationship most similar to: FRUGAL : EXTRAVAGANT a) Generous : Miserly b)

Honest : Deceitful c) Brave : Cowardly d) Happy : Sad

279. Select the word that is opposite in meaning to "ambiguous": a) Vague b) Unclear c) Definite d) Equivocal

280. Choose the word that does not belong in the group: a) Euphoric b) Ecstatic c) Elated d) Despondent

281. Identify the word that best completes the sentence: The mountain climber's _____ attitude helped him overcome numerous obstacles. a) pessimistic b) defeatist c) indomitable d) submissive

282. Select the pair of words with the relationship most similar to: OMNIVORE : DIET a) Polyglot : Language b) Bibliophile : Books c) Philanthropist : Charity d) Misanthrope : People

283. Choose the word with the closest meaning to "pernicious": a) Beneficial b) Harmless c) Detrimental d) Innocuous

284. Identify the word that is opposite in meaning to "perfidious": a) Treacherous b) Loyal c) Deceitful d) Unfaithful

285. Select the word that does not belong in the group: a) Altruistic b) Selfless c) Philanthropic d) Egocentric

CONTACT THE AUTHOR

I always strive to make this guide as comprehensive and helpful as possible, but there's always room for improvement. If you have any questions, suggestions, or feedback, I would love to hear from you. Hearing your thoughts helps me understand what works, what doesn't, and what could be made better in future editions.
To make it easier for you to reach out, I have set up a dedicated email address:
 epicinkpublishing@gmail.com

Feel free to email me for:

- Clarifications on any topics covered in this book

- Suggestions for additional topics or improvements

- Feedback on your experience with the book

- Any problem (You can't get the bonuses for example, please before releasing a negative review, contact me)

Your input is invaluable.

I read every email and will do my best to respond in a timely manner.

GET YOUR BONUSES

Dear reader,

First and foremost, thank you for purchasing my book!
Your support means the world to me, and I hope you find
the information within valuable and helpful in your
journey.

As a token of my appreciation, I have included
some exclusive bonuses that will greatly benefit you.
To access these bonuses, scan the QR Code with your
phone:

Once again, thank you for your support, and I wish you the
best of luck in your Exam. I believe these bonuses will
provide you with the tools and knowledge to excel.

Made in United States
North Haven, CT
24 November 2024

60892341R00165